HALIBUT

THE COOKBOOK

HALIBUT

THE COOKBOOK

edited by

KAREN BARNABY

whitecap

First printing, 2007

Edited by Ben D'Andrea
Proofread by Nadine Boyd
Cover and interior design by Jacqui Thomas
Typeset by Five Seventeen
Food photography by Tracy Kusiewicz and food styling by Irene McGuinness, unless otherwise noted
Cover photography by Tracy Kusiewicz
Illustrations by Heather Horton

Printed and bound in Canada by Friesens

LIBRARY AND ARCHIVES CANADA CATALOGUING IN PUBLICATION

Halibut : the cookbook / Karen Barnaby, editor.

Includes index.
ISBN-13: 978-1-55285-860-8
ISBN-10: 1-55285-860-X

1. Cookery (Halibut) I. Barnaby, Karen

TX747.H33 2007   641.6'92   C2006-905199-2

The publisher acknowledges the financial support of the Government of Canada through the Book Publishing Industry Development Program for our publishing activities.

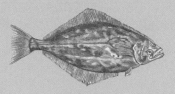

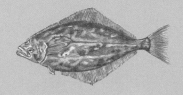

INTRODUCTION

HALIBUT IS ALL ABOUT ELEGANT TEXTURE, appearance, and sweet, subtle flavor. I love to tease a fillet apart into large, silky flakes. And simple is best. My favorite way to eat it is with lemon butter and a sprinkling of chives. I keep it away from the grill because it takes away some of its purity. But my feelings for halibut weren't always like this.

I grew up on rectangular, frozen fish. Every Friday morning the blue High Liner box was left on the counter to thaw. Before dinner, the fillets were placed in a glass baking dish and baked. Haddock, cod, or sole looked the same, was cooked the same, and tasted the same—"same" meaning white, overcooked, and bland. I reached for the ketchup bottle every time the plate of dry white fish appeared before me. We did have the occasional fish stick dinner, which was much better. We had no salmon, except for canned—and certainly no halibut.

I discovered halibut when I moved to Toronto, barely giving it a nod. My focus was on monkfish, tuna, squid, and whole small bony fish like red snapper, mackerel, and mullet. All things Italian had burst onto the food scene, and whole fish were the "it" fish, sizzling off the grill with fresh herbs and extra virgin olive oil. Grilled squid and firm medallions of monkfish appeared in almost every menu. Everything safe to eat raw—there were some dubious things—was made into carpaccio.

Halibut gently nudged me when I moved to Vancouver, but it still didn't stir my heart. I barely gave it a chance and thought it was a bland fish for people who don't like fish. I was enamored with sablefish and skate. Sablefish was the bad boy who rode the Harley. Skate was edgy. If skate were human, it would have tattoos and multiple body piercings. Halibut was a sissy—too pristine to get my attention. Though I wasn't crazy about halibut fillets, I did love the cheeks. They had what I thought was at least a shred of character.

As fate would have it—cooking thousands of pounds of it did help—I slowly learned to love halibut's simplicity. It didn't have to be bad to be good.

COOKING HALIBUT
What to Look For

When choosing halibut, look for firm, translucent flesh. Halibut shouldn't smell fishy but have a mild briny scent. Avoid halibut with a chalky appearance. The flesh will be soft and stringy after it's cooked.

It's rare to find whole halibut for sale. Instead, we have easy-to-deal-with steaks and fillets. Halibut fillets can be cut cleanly from the bone with a sharp boning knife.

halibut fillet

halibut steak

How to Store It

Store halibut (or any fish) on ice, refrigerated. Make sure that it's well wrapped and sitting on top of the ice. Use a deep container and change the ice as it melts.

Halibut's season is almost nine months, so I prefer to use it fresh. The short time that it isn't available makes the heart grow fonder. If you choose frozen halibut, let it thaw completely in the fridge before cooking it.

Freezing fresh halibut at home isn't recommended. The low temperature of a home freezer—as opposed to a commercial freezer—causes the fish to freeze slowly, creating ruptured cells. When the fish thaws, it releases more liquid because of the ruptured cells. The halibut will be dry, its texture compromised.

How to Cook It

Halibut is a lean fish and not as forgiving as fattier fish such as salmon or sablefish, so timing is crucial. There are no rules for cooking time. It depends on the thickness of the fish, cooking method, and your utensils. The fillet should look moist and should feel firm but slightly springy to the touch. It's okay to check if it's done to your liking by piercing the center. A meat thermometer should show an internal temperature between 140° to 145°F (60° to 63°F).

Grilling works well for thin fillets or steaks. Place the fish on a greased grill. Lightly flouring then oiling the fish will prevent it from sticking. You can also baste the fish with a marinade as it grills, and turn the fish once, halfway through cooking. Available in gourmet cookware shops, fish baskets make it easy to turn the fish over on the grill.

Broiling is a good choice for thick fillets. Place the fillets in a single layer on a well-oiled pan about 4 inches from the heat. Season the fish with salt, pepper, and herbs, if you wish, and baste it during cooking with a flavorful liquid or fat. Olive oil, butter, white wine, or lemon juice will enhance the flavor. Turn once, halfway through cooking.

Baking is good for small steaks and fillets. Arrange the fish in a well-oiled dish and drizzle with lemon juice, olive oil or butter, white wine, and/or broth and a sprinkling of herbs, salt, and pepper. Cook in a preheated 400°F (200°C) oven for 8 to 10 minutes, depending on thickness.

Sautéing is ideal for thin fillets. If you prefer, you can lightly flour the fish. Season with salt, pepper, and herbs if desired. Heat oil or clarified butter over medium heat in a heavy frying pan. Turn once, halfway through cooking.

Pan roasting makes a nice crispy crust on halibut and looks appealing. Preheat the oven to 350°F (180°C). Then heat ¼ inch (6 mm) of oil or clarified butter in a heavy frying pan over high heat. (It doesn't have to be a non-stick pan, just non-sticky.) Season the fillets and place in the pan. Turn the heat to medium and watch for a golden brown crust to develop around the edges. Place the pan in the oven and bake for 8 to 10 minutes, depending on the thickness. Remove the pan from the oven and serve the fish crispy side up.

Poaching works for steaks and fillets. Cook them in a simmering liquid—fish broth, vegetable broth, wine, or a combination of wine and water. Poached fish is often served cold or at room temperature with cold sauce, such as herbed mayonnaise, yogurt, sour cream, or a vinaigrette.

two-tiered aluminum steamer

Steaming is a great choice for halibut fillets. I prefer using a large, tiered Asian-style aluminum steamer. Use only an inch or two of water for steaming and bring to a full boil. Place the fillets on a plate and season heavily because the flavors will be diluted with water. Asian flavors work well here; fermented black beans, ginger, sake, sesame oil, soy sauce, and green onions are all good choices. Cooking will take around 8 to 10 minutes, depending on the thickness of the fillet. Remove from the steamer and serve immediately.

traditional two-tiered bamboo steamer

Flavors for Halibut

Halibut's neutral flavor makes it an ideal fish for many different seasonings. Basil, tarragon, mint, lemon grass, thyme, and oregano all enhance halibut. If you use fresh basil, add it after cooking to preserve its flavor. Spices such as cumin, fennel, coriander seeds, chilies, and curry powder work well too.

Halibut can be seasoned with herbs and spices before cooking, but don't let halibut sit in any form of acid for longer than 1 hour before cooking. The acid "cooks" the flesh and will make the halibut tough.

Right before cooking, you can add a splash of wine, lemon juice, clam nectar, or olive oil.

After cooking, a sprinkling of lemon juice or flavored vinegars and oils will add another dimension of taste. And butter seems to be a natural with halibut.

Halibut Nutritional Content

Halibut is an excellent protein source as well as a good source of potassium and omega-3 fatty acids.

BONELESS HALIBUT (COOKED) Serving Size 4 oz (100 g)
Total Fat 3.33 g
Saturated Fat 0.473 g
Polyunsaturated Fat 1.07 g
Monounsaturated Fat 1.1 g
Cholesterol 46.47 mg
Omega-3 Fatty Acids 0.62 g
Total Carbohydrate 0 g
Dietary Fiber 0 g
Protein 30.25 g
Sodium 78.2 mg
Potassium 652.8 mg

APPETIZERS

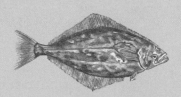

THE PACIFIC HALIBUT
(HIPPOGLOSSUS STENOLEPIS)

The name derives from the Greek hippo *(horse),*
glossa *(tongue),* steno *(narrow), and* lepis *(scale).*
In English, hali *signifies holy, and* but *denotes flat.*

᷉

Make a fish stock to start this elegant fish chowder, using the bones reserved from filleting your fish. Any extra stock can be frozen to use in future soups and sauces. Serves 6

HALIBUT CHOWDER

INGREDIENTS

¼ cup	butter	60 mL
3 Tbsp	all-purpose flour	45 mL
6 cups	fish stock (see page 176)	1.5 L
1 cup	finely diced carrots	250 mL
½ cup	finely diced parsnips	125 mL
½ cup	cleaned and finely sliced leeks, white part only	125 mL
1 lb	boneless, skinless halibut, cubed	500 g
2	egg yolks	2
to taste	salt and freshly ground black pepper	to taste
½ cup	sour cream	125 mL
3 Tbsp	minced parsley	45 mL

METHOD

In a large saucepan over medium-low heat, melt the butter and whisk in the flour. Cook for 1 minute, then slowly whisk in the stock. Stir until the mixture comes to a boil and thickens slightly. Add the carrots, parsnips, and leeks. Simmer for 10 more minutes, then add the fish. Cook for 5 minutes or until the halibut turns translucent.

In a small bowl, beat the egg yolks. Whisk in a little of the hot soup broth, 3 Tbsp (45 mL) at a time, just to heat the eggs. Remove the soup from the heat and stir in the eggs. Season with salt and pepper to taste. Serve immediately in wide, shallow bowls. Garnish with a dollop of sour cream and the parsley.

You can use Indian candy in place of the smoked salmon. Serves 4

HALIBUT CHOWDER
WITH SMOKED SALMON & DILL

INGREDIENTS

3 Tbsp	butter	45 mL
1	medium onion, finely chopped	1
2	celery stalks, finely chopped	2
1	clove garlic, finely chopped	1
3 Tbsp	flour	45 mL
3 cups	chicken or fish stock (see page 176)	750 mL
1	bay leaf	1
2	medium red-skinned potatoes, cut into small cubes	2
1	4-oz (100-g) package cold smoked salmon, chopped	1
1 lb	halibut fillets, skinned and cut into small cubes	500 g
1 cup	light cream	250 mL
1 Tbsp	chopped fresh dill	15 mL
to taste	salt and white pepper	to taste

METHOD

Melt the butter in a pot over medium heat. Add the onion, celery, and garlic and cook until tender, about 5 minutes. Sprinkle in the flour and mix well. Slowly stir in the stock. Bring to a boil, and then reduce the heat to a gentle simmer. Add the bay leaf, potatoes, smoked salmon, and halibut and cook until the potatoes are just tender, about 10 to 15 minutes. Stir in the cream and dill and gently simmer a few minutes more. Season with salt and pepper and serve.

Ceviche is a traditional raw/marinated Latin American fish dish. It's very important to use only the freshest, highest quality fish. The raw fish is marinated in citrus juice, herbs, and spices. The citric acid produces a mild pickling effect, inhibiting bacterial growth, "cooking" the flesh, removing the raw fish flavor, and turning the flesh opaque. Serves 4

HALIBUT, FENNEL & GARLIC CEVICHE

INGREDIENTS

1 tsp	minced garlic	5 mL
1	lime, juice and zest	1
1	lemon, juice and zest	1
½ cup	white wine	125 mL
1 Tbsp	honey	15 mL
1 tsp	minced jalapeño pepper, seeds removed	5 mL
1 Tbsp	chopped fresh cilantro	15 mL
1 Tbsp	chopped fresh fennel leaves	15 mL
to taste	salt and black pepper	to taste
1 lb	fresh halibut, cut into thin slices	500 g
1	bulb fennel, cut in paper-thin slices	1
for garnish	additional cilantro sprigs	for garnish

METHOD

Place the garlic, lime juice and zest, lemon juice and zest, white wine, honey, jalapeño, chopped cilantro, and fennel leaves in a non-reactive (preferably glass) bowl. Stir well and season with salt and pepper.

Add the sliced halibut and fennel, tossing gently to mix. Cover with plastic wrap and chill for at least 1 hour (to a maximum of 6 hours). Just before serving, toss gently and garnish with cilantro sprigs. Serve chilled or at room temperature.

This dish works especially well in early summer when Pacific shrimp, local halibut, and young, garden-fresh zucchini are available. Serves 6

HALIBUT & SHRIMP CAKES
WITH GINGERED ZUCCHINI MARMALADE

INGREDIENTS

10 oz	halibut fillet	300 g
	olive oil for drizzling	
5 oz	baby shrimp, cooked and peeled	150 g
2 cups	panko (Japanese bread crumbs available at Asian markets)	500 mL
2 Tbsp	sliced fresh chives	30 mL
½	fennel bulb, finely diced	½
5 Tbsp	mayonnaise	75 mL
to taste	kosher salt and freshly ground black pepper	to taste
	vegetable oil for frying	

continues on next page

METHOD

Preheat the oven to 375°F (190°C). Place the halibut on a baking sheet, drizzle with olive oil, and bake until flaky, about 15 minutes. Set aside to cool, then place in a large bowl and flake. Add the shrimp, 1 cup (250 mL) of the panko, the chives, and fennel. Mix well. Blend in the mayonnaise. Season with salt and pepper, then form the mixture into 4-inch (10-cm) cakes that are about ½ inch (1 cm) thick. Place the remaining 1 cup (250 mL) of panko in a small bowl. Roll the cakes in the panko.

Heat ½ inch (1 cm) of the vegetable oil in a large frying pan over medium heat. Brown the cakes on both sides, heating them through. Serve with the zucchini marmalade.

Gingered Zucchini Marmalade

Makes about 4 cups (1 L)

2¼ lb	zucchini, diced	1 kg
2	lemons	2
2	oranges	2
1	3-inch (8-cm) piece fresh ginger, grated	1
1	apple, quartered and cored	1
4¼ cups	sugar	1 L

Place the diced zucchini in a stainless steel pot. Zest the lemons and oranges and add the zest to the zucchini. Peel the citrus pith (the white underlying part of the citrus fruit) and place the pith and grated ginger in a piece of cheesecloth. Tie it up to make a sachet bag.

Purée the apple and peeled lemons and oranges in a food processor and add the zucchini, along with the sugar. Place the cheesecloth bag in the pot. Bring to a boil, stirring well. Reduce the heat to low and simmer for 45 minutes. Remove the cheese cloth bag. If you wish, purée, using a hand blender or food processor, and set aside to cool.

Leftover marmalade will keep in the refrigerator for 6 to 8 weeks.

A small green salad beside the cakes adds color and texture to the plate. Makes 12 (2-inch/5-cm) cakes

HALIBUT & SMOKED SALMON CAKES
WITH ROMESCO SAUCE & LEMON MAYONNAISE

INGREDIENTS

20 oz	halibut fillets, cut in ¼-inch (6-mm) dice	600 g
6 oz	smoked salmon, thinly sliced and minced	175 g
4 Tbsp	finely minced red onion	60 mL
2 tsp	finely minced garlic	10 mL
2 tsp	capers, minced	10 mL
1 Tbsp	minced fresh jalapeño pepper	15 mL
2 Tbsp	minced chives	30 mL
1–2	eggs	1–2
2–3 Tbsp	lemon juice	30–45 mL
to taste	kosher salt	to taste
¼ tsp	freshly ground white pepper	1 mL
2–3 cups	breadcrumbs	500–750 mL
3–4 Tbsp	olive oil	45–60 mL
3–4 Tbsp	unsalted butter	45–60 mL

continues on next page

METHOD

If time is of the essence, mince the onion, garlic, capers, jalapeño pepper, and chives in a mini food processor. Always cut the fish by hand.

Preheat the oven to 400°F (200°C). Put the halibut, smoked salmon, onion, garlic, capers, jalapeño pepper, and chives in a bowl and toss gently. Lightly whisk 1 egg. Add the egg, lemon juice, salt and pepper, and toss again. The mixture should be fairly loose. Add more lemon juice and another egg if it seems too dry.

Put the breadcrumbs in a shallow bowl. Shape the halibut mixture into 12 discs. Cover all the sides with breadcrumbs. The cakes will be very delicate and moist.

Melt 1 Tbsp (15 mL) oil and 1 Tbsp (15 mL) butter in a non-stick frying pan. When just sizzling, add the cakes. Brown on both sides, turning gently to prevent the cakes from breaking. Add more oil and butter as needed.

Remove to a baking tray. Bake in the oven for 10 minutes. Serve immediately with a spoonful of

Romesco Sauce

Makes about 2 cups (500 mL)

3	roasted red peppers (see sidebar)	3
2	large cloves garlic, coarsely chopped	2
2	slices white bread, crusts removed, lightly toasted, sliced ¾ inch (2 cm) thick and cut into 1-inch (2.5-cm) cubes	2
pinch	cayenne pepper	pinch
¼ tsp	kosher salt	1 mL
pinch	freshly ground white pepper	pinch
¾ cup	olive oil	175 mL

continues on next page

Romesco Sauce on the side and a drizzle of Lemon Mayonnaise overtop.

Romesco Sauce

Put the roasted red peppers, garlic, bread, cayenne, salt, and pepper in a food processor. Process in bursts, scraping down the bowl in between until the ingredients are well combined. With the machine running, slowly drizzle in ½ cup (125 mL) of the oil. Check for seasoning and consistency. The sauce should be thick enough to just hold its shape on a spoon. Add the extra oil if necessary.

ROASTED RED PEPPERS

To roast bell peppers, grill or broil the whole peppers, turning often to ensure the sides are evenly charred. Place them in a brown paper bag and let them cool. Steaming them like this makes the peppers much easier to peel. Use your fingers to peel off the skin, and discard the stem and seeds.

Lemon Mayonnaise
Makes about 1½ cups (375 mL)

1 tsp	Dijon mustard	5 mL
1	egg	1
1 cup	corn or canola oil	250 mL
3 Tbsp	lemon juice	45 mL
¼ tsp	kosher salt, heaping	1 mL
pinch	freshly ground black pepper	pinch

Lemon Mayonnaise

Put the mustard in a bowl and whisk in the egg. Dribble the oil very slowly into the egg, whisking continuously. If the whisking makes your arm tired, take a break. The mixture won't separate.

When all the oil is incorporated, start adding the lemon juice ½ tsp (2 mL) at a time. Continue to whisk. Taste after each addition. Add salt and pepper to taste.

If this method seems too daunting, put the mustard and egg in a food processor and pulse to blend. With the processor on, slowly pour in the oil. When the mixture has emulsified, add the lemon juice, salt, and pepper. Mayonnaise made in the food processor will be thicker than mayonnaise whisked by hand.

Cover and keep in the refrigerator until ready to use.

Crabmeat, smoked salmon, and shrimp combine to give these melts a sumptuous taste. Makes 24 melts

SUMPTUOUS SEAFOOD MELTS

INGREDIENTS

1	8-oz (250-g) package firm cream cheese, at room temperature	1
¼ cup	mayonnaise	60 mL
1	clove garlic, finely chopped	1
½ tsp	hot pepper sauce	2 mL
5 oz	crabmeat	150 g
2 oz	cold-smoked salmon, coarsely chopped	50 g
2 tsp	chopped fresh dill or tarragon, plus some sprigs for garnish	10 mL
to taste	salt, white pepper, and freshly squeezed lemon juice	to taste
1	baguette, cut into 24 rounds, ¼ inch (5 mm) thick	1
1 cup	cooked, flaked halibut	250 mL
1 cup	shredded Swiss cheese	250 mL

METHOD

Preheat the oven to 425°F (220°C). Line a baking sheet with parchment paper. Place the cream cheese in a large bowl and beat with an electric mixer until soft and lightened. Mix in the mayonnaise, garlic, and hot pepper sauce and beat until smooth. Stir in the crab, salmon, dill or tarragon, salt, pepper, and lemon juice. Spread the seafood mixture on the baguette slices and place on the baking sheet. Decorate the top of each melt with the halibut and sprinkle with the cheese. Bake for 10 to 12 minutes, or until the cheese is melted and lightly golden on top. Arrange on a serving platter, garnish each melt with a dill or tarragon sprig, and serve immediately.

ERIC'S TIP

These melts, unbaked, can be made several hours in advance and stored in the fridge until needed. Because the melts will be cold, add a few minutes to the baking time.

Halibut's firm, perfectly white flesh makes it spectacular in any recipe. I love these meaty skewers because they excite the eye and the palate with festive colors and tropical flavors. Makes 8 hors d'oeuvres

HALIBUT KEBABS

INGREDIENTS

For the marinade

1	lime, juice of	1
2 Tbsp	vegetable oil	30 mL
2 Tbsp	chopped fresh basil	30 mL
1	clove garlic, finely minced	1
½ tsp	dried red chili flakes, or to taste	2 mL

continues on next page

METHOD

Combine the marinade ingredients in a non-reactive bowl. Cut the halibut into 24 equal pieces (2 cuts lengthwise, 3 cuts across) and toss with the marinade. Marinate for 20 minutes to 1 hour, but no longer.

Assemble 12 skewers, alternating chunks of fish and vegetables with the mango and pineapple (mango-fish-pineapple-fish-onion-fish).

Preheat the grill on medium-high for 5 to 10 minutes or until the chamber temperature rises above 500°F (260°C). Rinse the planks and place them on the cooking grate. Cover the grill and heat the planks for 4 or 5 minutes, or until they start to throw off a bit of smoke and crackle lightly. Reduce the heat to medium.

Place the kebabs on the planks. Cook for 12 to 15 minutes, turning once or twice, until the fish chunks are springy to the touch. Season with a sprinkling of salt, a drizzle of oil, and serve 2 to a plate. Garnish with lime wedges and basil sprigs.

For the fish

1	cedar plank, soaked overnight or at least 1 hour	1
1 lb	boneless, skinless halibut fillet, about ¾ inch (1.5 cm) thick	500 g
12	7-inch (18-cm) bamboo skewers, soaked for at least 1 hour	12
2	ripe mangoes, peeled, cored, and cut into 12 bite-sized chunks	2
½	ripe pineapple, peeled, cored, and cut into 12 bite-sized chunks	½
1	red onion, cut into 12 bite-sized chunks	1
to taste	kosher salt and freshly ground black pepper	to taste
	olive oil for drizzling	
for garnish	lime wedges and basil sprigs	for garnish

Halibut is delicious with bacon and cabbage. The light, creamy herb sauce makes it divine. Serves 6

LINGUINI WITH HALIBUT, BACON & CABBAGE

INGREDIENTS

2 slices	side bacon, minced	2 slices
1 lb	halibut fillets cut into 1-inch (2.5-cm) cubes	500 g
1	washed and trimmed leek, white and light green part only, thinly sliced	1
1 Tbsp	puréed ginger root	15 mL
6	cloves garlic, minced	6
⅔ cup	shredded finely Savoy cabbage	150 mL
1	lemon, juice and zest	1
½ cup	dry white wine	125 mL
1 cup	fish stock (see page 176), mild chicken stock, or clam nectar	250 mL
1 Tbsp	cornstarch	15 mL
¼ cup	whipping cream	60 mL
1 Tbsp	minced fresh thyme	15 mL
1 Tbsp	minced fresh tarragon	15 mL
to taste	salt and hot chili flakes	to taste
18 oz	linguini	525 g
for garnish	chive sprigs	for garnish

METHOD

In a large, non-stick sauté pan, cook the bacon until well done. Remove the bacon and discard virtually all the fat from the pan, leaving no more than 2 to 3 tsp (10 to 15 mL). Reheat the pan and add the halibut in a single layer. Using tongs to turn the pieces, brown the halibut over high heat, removing it to a plate or bowl as soon as it loses its translucent quality.

Return the pan to the stove, adding the leek, ginger, and garlic. Cook over high heat until tender, adding water as needed to prevent the vegetables from burning. Add the shredded cabbage, lemon, and white wine. Bring to a boil, then add the fish stock.

Dissolve the cornstarch in a little cold water. Return the reserved bacon to the pan, bring the liquid to a boil, and stir in the cornstarch. Boil briefly until the sauce is clear, then stir in the whipping cream, herbs, and halibut. Taste, adding salt, hot chili flakes, and lemon juice as needed to balance the flavors.

Cook the pasta in salted boiling water. Drain it well, then toss in the pan with the sauce. Serve hot, garnished with chive sprigs.

When you need a dish to impress a date or your spouse, try this. It's simple to make, but fancy in appearance and taste. *Serves 4*

SEAFOOD SAMPLER

INGREDIENTS

4	2 oz (50 g) halibut fillets	4
4	large sea scallops	4
4	large shrimp, peeled, with tail portion intact	4
4	medium oysters, shucked and left in the half shell	4
¼ cup	dry white wine	60 mL
2–3 Tbsp	melted butter	30–45 mL
1 Tbsp	chopped fresh tarragon, or 1 tsp (5 mL) dried	15 mL
1	clove garlic, finely chopped	1
pinch	paprika and cayenne pepper	pinch
to taste	salt, freshly ground pepper, and lemon juice	to taste
2 Tbsp	grated Parmesan cheese	30 mL
to garnish	lemon wedges	to garnish

METHOD

Preheat the oven to 450°F (230°C). Place the halibut, scallops, shrimp, and oysters in a single layer in a shallow baking dish. Combine the wine, butter, tarragon, garlic, paprika, cayenne, salt, pepper, and lemon juice in a bowl. Drizzle over the seafood. Sprinkle the Parmesan cheese over the oysters. Bake for 12–15 minutes, or until the seafood is just cooked. Serve straight out of the baking dish, or arrange on plates, spooning the pan juices over top. Garnish with lemon wedges.

ERIC'S TIP

This dish can be made oven-ready hours in advance. Cover and refrigerate until you're ready to bake and serve. You can also use dill or parsley instead of tarragon.

Halibut is perfect in this creamy, delicious dip. Makes 1½ cups (375 mL)

HOT HALIBUT DIP

INGREDIENTS

¼ cup	mayonnaise	60 mL
1	8-oz (225-g) package cream cheese, softened	1
½ tsp	cayenne pepper	2 mL
¼ tsp	salt	1 mL
pinch	pepper	pinch
½ lb	cooked halibut fillet, flaked	250 g
¼ cup	finely chopped green onions	60 mL
2 Tbsp	chopped fresh parsley	30 mL

METHOD

Preheat the oven to 350°F (180°C). Beat the mayonnaise, cream cheese, cayenne, salt, and pepper in a food processor or with an electric mixer, until creamy. Fold in the halibut and green onions. Mix well. Transfer to a medium baking dish.

Bake for 20 minutes, or until bubbly and heated through. Sprinkle with the parsley just before serving.

MARISA'S TIP

The dip can be assembled a day in advance. Cover and refrigerate until you're ready to bake it.

GENTLY SIMMERED, POACHED
& STEAMED

Halibut are longer than most flatfish,
their length being three times more
than their width.

◦

The color on the top side of the halibut varies but
tends to mimic the color of the ocean floor.
The underside is usually white, appearing more like
the sky from below. This color adaptation allows
halibut to avoid detection by prey and from predators.

◦

Serve this light and healthy dish with steamed long-grain, jasmine, or basmati rice, and dinner is ready. If you can't find fresh shiitake mushrooms, replace them with an equal amount of medium white or brown mushrooms cut in half. Serves 2

CURRIED STEAMED HALIBUT
WITH ASIAN-STYLE VEGETABLES

INGREDIENTS

2	5- to 6-oz (150- to 175-g) halibut fillets	2
1 Tbsp	mild, medium, or hot curry paste	15 mL
2–3	baby bok choy, trimmed and separated into leaves	2–3
10	snow or snap peas, trimmed	10
8	baby corn	8
1	small red pepper, halved and cubed	1
1	small carrot, cut in thin diagonal slices	1
6–8	fresh shiitake mushrooms, stems removed	6–8
1 Tbsp	sesame seeds, toasted	15 mL
2 Tbsp	chopped cilantro or green onion	30 mL

METHOD

Rub or brush the halibut fillets with curry paste. Cover and marinate in the fridge, if time allows, for 1 hour. Line a bamboo steamer with bok choy leaves (the steamer I use is 11 inches/28 cm in diameter). Set the fish in the steamer. Artfully arrange the peas, corn, red pepper, carrot, and mushrooms around the fish. Place the lid on the steamer and set in a wok, skillet, or pot filled with boiling water to a level just below the steamer. Steam for 10 minutes or until the fish and vegetables are just cooked through. Serve from the steamer, garnished with the cilantro or green onion.

The wrapping medium is your choice. If your garden produces prodigious amounts of beet greens, use them. Or wilt Savoy cabbage, try Chinese greens, leek tops, sorrel leaves, or big spinach leaves. Serves 4

HALIBUT WRAPPED IN SPINACH
WITH BLACK BEAN STEAM

INGREDIENTS

4	5-oz (150-g) halibut fillets	4
1	bunch large-leaf spinach, chard, sorrel, or other firm green	1
2 cups	Black Bean Sauce	500 mL

continues on next page

DEE'S TIP

If all the fussing, wilting, and wrapping is more than you can face, pan-steam the fish; set it aside, covered, and quickly wilt the greens in the same pan. Turn the greens onto a platter, drizzle with the sauce, top with the fish and more sauce, and then sprinkle with sesame seeds to garnish. For an extra bite of flavor, add strands of pickled ginger for garnish.

METHOD

Trim the fillets into tidy pieces of even thickness. Wash the greens and discard the stems. In a large non-stick sauté pan, quickly cook the greens over high heat, using just the water clinging to the leaves and turning the greens over several times with tongs. Cook just long enough to wilt. Spinach will take mere seconds, while the chard leaves with take longer.

Spread the wilted leaves out flat on the cutting board, overlapping the edges to form a wrapper large enough to encase each fillet. Wrap the fillets in the greens, tucking the ends under to form tidy packages. Pour the black bean sauce into the sauté pan and bring to a boil. Place the wrapped fish packages in the sauce, cover, and steam over medium-high heat until just done, allowing about 8 minutes per inch (2.5 cm) of thickness. If you're in doubt, remove the largest fillet and use a small sharp knife to slit a small hole in the center to check for doneness.

Black Bean Sauce
Makes 3–4 cups (750 mL–1 L)

1	onion, minced	1
1	leek, minced	1
1	red bell pepper, minced	1
1 Tbsp	canola oil	15 mL
2 Tbsp	puréed ginger root	30 mL
2 Tbsp	puréed garlic	30 mL
1	orange, juice and zest	1
½ cup	dry white wine or sake	125 mL
¾ cup	hoisin sauce	175 mL
2 Tbsp	lemon juice	30 mL
1–2 cups	water	250–500 mL
2 Tbsp	soy sauce	30 mL
to taste	hot chili flakes	to taste
2 Tbsp	dried, fermented black beans	30 mL
2	green onions, minced	2
2 Tbsp	minced cilantro	30 mL
1 Tbsp	sesame oil	15 mL

To serve, ladle a quarter of the sauce onto each large, shallow bowl or plate and arrange a wrapped fillet on top. Sprinkle with sesame seeds. Serve with basmati rice, plain rice noodles, or egg noodles.

Black Bean Sauce

Sauté the onion, leek, and red pepper in the oil, cooking them until tender. Add the remaining ingredients, except the green onions, cilantro, and sesame oil. Simmer for several minutes, until the flavors are friendly and it's reduced and thickened to the desired texture—slightly thicker for pizza, thinner for a steaming sauce. Remove from the heat and add the remaining ingredients.

DEE'S TIP

Black bean sauce is classic, a staple of southern Chinese cuisine, and it deserves to be eaten in every household in the world. I use this basted on ribs, steamed with mussels and clams, brushed onto grilled fish, with whole crab, and as a sauce on pizza, pasta, and barbecued duck or pork. It keeps well, so make extra and store it in the refrigerator for up to a week. If you're tempted to make vats of it, leave out the fresh herbs and add them when you use the sauce.

This technique of poaching white fish in red wine may seem unconventional, and will probably raise a few eyebrows. But, the dramatic presentation and lovely flavor are unforgettable. The key to this recipe is to use super-fresh halibut; any sign of fishiness from taste to smell will upset the balance of this recipe. Serves 6

HALIBUT POACHED IN RED WINE

INGREDIENTS

2 Tbsp	unsalted butter, divided	30 mL
1 Tbsp	olive oil	15 mL
1	bay leaf	1
2 tsp	mustard seeds	10 mL
2 tsp	white peppercorns	10 mL
2	shallots, finely diced	2
½ cup	carrot, finely chopped	125 mL
½ cup	celery, finely chopped	125 mL
½ cup	shiitake mushrooms, finely chopped	125 mL
2	tomatoes, seeded and finely chopped	2
2 Tbsp	honey	30 mL
3 cups	Cabernet Sauvignon	750 mL
1 cup	fish stock (see page 176)	250 mL
2 Tbsp	verjus (or red wine vinegar)	30 mL
to taste	kosher salt and white pepper	to taste

continues on next page

METHOD

Heat a saucepan over medium heat and add 1 Tbsp (15 mL) butter and the oil. When the butter has completely melted, add the bay leaf, mustard seeds, and white peppercorns. Add the shallots, carrot, celery, shiitake mushroom, and tomatoes.

Cook, stirring frequently, for about 5 minutes or until the vegetables begin to wilt slightly. Stir in the honey to coat the vegetables. Add the wine, stock, and verjus. Bring to a boil and reduce the liquid to about 1 cup (250 mL).

Reduce the heat to a simmer. Season the halibut with salt and pepper and add to the stock. Poach for 7 minutes or until the fish is opaque. With a slotted spoon, remove the halibut from the poaching liquid and reserve.

Strain the liquid through a sieve into a bowl and discard the vegetables. Increase the heat, return the liquid to the saucepan, and bring it to a boil. Reduce the liquid until just ½ cup (125 mL) remains. Add the remaining 1 Tbsp (15 mL) of butter and stir until it melts.

To blanch lemon zest, you first need to zest the lemons. A zester is a tool with several small holes at the top that makes long shreds when scraped along the rind of citrus fruits. Start at the top of the lemon and keep the pressure even while pressing down to create long shreds. You can also use it on hard vegetables such as carrots or cucumbers.

Once you have your zest, bring a small pot of water to a boil. Add the zest. When the water returns to a boil, drain the zest through a sieve and cool under cold water. Drain well, remove from the sieve, and place on paper towels to dry.

INGREDIENTS — continued

2 lb	halibut fillets, divided into 6 portions	1 kg
2	lemons, zest of, blanched	2
1 Tbsp	Italian parsley, finely chopped	15 mL
1 Tbsp	capers, rinsed and finely chopped	15 mL
1 tsp	fleur de sel	5 mL

METHOD — continued

Return the halibut to the pan and spoon the reduced liquid over top. Cook for 2 to 3 minutes or until the halibut is warmed through. Combine the lemon zest, parsley, capers, and fleur de sel in a small pile on top of the halibut.

Place the fish on warm serving plates and drizzle with the red wine glaze to serve.

Halibut looks stunning surrounded by this black bean vinaigrette. The halibut can be served chilled in the summer. Serves 4

POACHED HALIBUT
WITH GINGER & BLACK BEAN VINAIGRETTE

INGREDIENTS

1 cup	white wine	250 mL
4	¼-inch (6-mm) slices of ginger, lightly crushed	4
1	star anise	1
1 Tbsp	sugar	15 mL
2	green onions, lightly crushed	2
2 tsp	sea salt	10 mL
1	whole dried chili pepper	1
4 cups	water	1 L
4	6-oz (175-g) halibut fillets	4

continues on next page

METHOD

Combine all the ingredients, except for the halibut, in a non-corrodible pan that will fit the halibut snugly. Bring to a boil, then simmer for 15 minutes, partially covered with a lid.

Slip the halibut fillets into the liquid and regulate the heat so the halibut poaches gently for 10 minutes. Remove from the liquid. If you wish to serve the halibut cold, cool to room temperature, then cover and refrigerate. (The halibut may be prepared 1 day in advance.) To serve hot, transfer to heated plates or a platter. Spoon the vinaigrette around the halibut and serve.

Ginger & Black Bean Vinaigrette

2	medium cloves garlic, minced	2
1 Tbsp	fresh ginger, minced	15 mL
½ cup	pickled ginger (Gari) (see sidebar on page 172)	125 mL
3 Tbsp	pickled ginger juice	45 mL
2 Tbsp	apple cider vinegar	30 mL
¾ tsp	sea salt	4 mL
3 Tbsp	sugar	45 mL
¼ cup	fermented black beans	60 mL
¾ cup	vegetable oil	175 mL

Ginger & Black Bean Vinaigrette

Make the vinaigrette at least one day before using. Combine all the ingredients, except for the vegetable oil, in a food processor or blender. Pulse until very finely chopped. With the motor running, add the vegetable oil in a slow, steady stream and process until well blended. Cover and refrigerate. The vinaigrette will keep for up to a week in the refrigerator. Bring it to room temperature before serving.

This dish—called *hor muk*—is usually served in small one-cup portions made out of a folded banana leaf. The filled banana-leaf cups are then placed in a bamboo steamer. The larger casserole version is more practical for Western kitchens. *Hor muk* is often made without the chilies as a food for young children. Serves 4

STEAMED HALIBUT CUSTARD

INGREDIENTS

¾ lb	halibut fillets	375 g
1½ cup	coconut milk, divided	375 mL
2 Tbsp	red curry paste	30 mL
2	eggs, lightly beaten	2
¼ lb	assorted seafood, such as prawns or scallops	125 g
1 Tbsp	fish sauce	15 mL
1 tsp	salt	5 mL
4	frozen banana leaves, about 12 × 14 inches (30 × 35 cm), defrosted	4
1 cup	Thai basil leaves	250 mL
1 Tbsp	rice flour	15 mL
2	kaffir lime leaves, finely shredded	2
2	red chilies, thinly sliced	2

METHOD

Preheat the oven to 400°F (200°C). Purée the halibut fillets in a food processor. Mix ¾ cup (175 mL) of the coconut milk with the curry paste. Add the fish purée and combine thoroughly. Stir in the eggs, seafood, fish sauce, and salt. Mix well.

Line a casserole dish with the banana leaves and scatter the basil leaves over the top of the banana leaves. Spoon the fish mixture over the basil leaves. Place the casserole dish in a baking pan filled with hot water, place it in the oven, and bake for 20 minutes.

Combine the remaining coconut milk with the rice flour and spread over the top of the seafood casserole. Sprinkle the lime leaves and red chili over the coconut rice flour topping and bake for another 5 minutes.

This makes a nice entrée for entertaining, but it's easy enough to pull off during the week. Serves 6

RIESLING BRAISED HALIBUT
WITH TARRAGON & CHIVES

INGREDIENTS

Poaching Liquid

1 cup	water	250 mL
1 cup	Riesling	250 mL
¾ cup	chopped onion	175 mL
½ cup	chopped celery	125 mL
1	lemon, sliced	1

Halibut

1 Tbsp	unsalted butter	15 mL
½	small onion, minced	½
6	6-oz (175-g) halibut fillets	6
to taste	coarse salt	to taste
1 Tbsp	chopped fresh tarragon	15 mL
2 Tbsp	thinly sliced chives	30 mL
1	lemon, cut in 6 wedges	1

METHOD

For the poaching liquid, bring the water and wine to a simmer with the onion, celery, and lemon. Simmer for 15 minutes. Strain out the vegetables and keep the liquid warm.

For the halibut, melt the butter in a large shallow pan over medium heat and sauté the onions until translucent, about 5 minutes. Season the fish with salt and add it to the pan. Add the poaching liquid and tarragon and simmer gently for 8 minutes or until the fish is firm to the touch and white in the center. Carefully remove it with a slotted spoon and top with the chives and a little of the poaching liquid. Serve with lemon wedges.

ANNA & MICHAEL'S TIP

For a rich chive sauce, reduce 1 cup (250 mL) of the poaching liquid with the juice of 1 lemon to a third of its volume. Remove from the heat and whisk in 2 Tbsp (30 mL) diced cold butter and 2 Tbsp (30 mL) chopped chives. Serve and do not reheat.

Similar to a classic bouillabaisse, this meal is served with a highly seasoned mayonnaise on the side.
Serves 6

HALIBUT & SEAFOOD HOTPOT
WITH SAFFRON AÏOLI

INGREDIENTS

2 Tbsp	vegetable oil	30 mL
1	small onion, julienned	1
1	celery stalk, diced	1
1	carrot, diced	1
2	cloves garlic, minced	2
1 cup	white wine	250 mL
3 cups	fish or shellfish stock (see page 176)	750 mL
1 lb	fresh mussels, debearded	500 g
8 oz	fresh halibut, diced	225 g
4 oz	tiger shrimp, deveined	100 g
4 oz	bay scallops	100 g
1 tsp	fresh thyme, chopped	5 mL
1	tomato, diced	1
1	potato, cooked, peeled, and diced	1
½ cup	corn or peas	125 mL
2 Tbsp	thinly sliced fresh basil	30 mL

METHOD

In a large saucepot, heat the oil and sauté the onion, celery, and carrot until tender, about 5 minutes. Add the garlic and sauté 1 minute more. Add the wine and stock, and bring to a simmer. Add the mussels; cover the pot, and simmer for 2 minutes. Add the halibut; cover, and simmer 2 minutes more. Then add the shrimp, scallops, thyme, tomato, potato, and corn. Simmer, covered, for another 2 to 3 minutes or until the mussels open. Add the basil, dill, salt, and pepper just before serving.

To prepare the aïoli, combine the saffron and lemon juice and let sit a few minutes to draw the flavor and color out of the saffron. Stir the mayonnaise and garlic into the saffron and lemon juice mixture.

To serve, ladle the hot pot into wide-mouthed soup bowls and spoon a dollop of aïoli directly on top. Or serve on the side slathered on toasted French bread, then dip the bread into the broth.

continues on next page

1 Tbsp	chopped fresh dill	15 mL
to taste	salt and pepper	to taste

Saffron Aïoli

pinch	saffron threads	pinch
1	lemon, juice of	1
¾ cup	mayonnaise	175 mL
2	cloves garlic, minced	2

My aunt Lila has spent most of her adult life living in the San Francisco Bay region. This is my version of her version of the Italian fishermen's stew that originated in the Bay area. Serves 6

LILA'S CIOPPINO

INGREDIENTS

1	onion, finely sliced	1
1	leek, white and light green part only, finely sliced	1
12	cloves garlic, minced	12
2	stalks celery, finely sliced	2
1	bulb fresh fennel, finely sliced	1
1 Tbsp	olive oil	15 mL
1 tsp	fennel seed, cracked	5 mL
1 tsp	dried basil	5 mL
1 tsp	dried oregano	5 mL
1 tsp	dried thyme	5 mL
1	bay leaf	1
pinch	saffron threads	pinch
1 Tbsp	cracked peppercorns	15 mL
1 cup	dry red wine	250 mL
1	lemon, juice and zest	1

continues on next page

METHOD

Make the sauce first; it can be made several days in advance and left to mellow in the fridge. In a large heavy-bottomed pan, cook the onion, leek, garlic, celery, and fennel with the olive oil, until the vegetables are tender, adding small amounts of water as needed. Stir in the dried herbs and spices, then add the red wine and bring to a boil. Stir in the lemon juice and zest, tomatoes, and tomato paste. Simmer until the sauce thickens and add the honey, salt, and pepper to balance the flavors. Cool, then cover and refrigerate.

On the day you plan to serve the cioppino, scrub the clams and mussels, pulling off and discarding any beards that protrude from the mussels. Cut the halibut into bite-sized pieces. Chop the crab into manageable lengths. Put large soup plates or bowls into the oven on low heat to warm up. Set out finger bowls of lemon-infused water, bowls for the shells, and copious

To determine how much fish to buy, calculate it per person: 4 shrimp or prawns, 4 clams, 4 mussels, 4 oz (100 g) crab in the shell, and 3 oz (75 g) firm-textured halibut. Buy and use shellfish in the shell; the flavor is better, and it contributes to the messy, hands-on casual feeling that conjures up crowded North Beach diners, counters strewn with wine glasses and bowls of shellfish. Cioppino doesn't reheat well—the fish tends to overcook, so cook only as much as can be eaten in one meal. Don't forget to buy several loaves of the best crusty sourdough bread you can find.

INGREDIENTS — continued

2	28-oz (796-mL) cans of Italian plum tomatoes	2
2 Tbsp	tomato paste	30 mL
2 Tbsp	honey	30 mL
to taste	salt and freshly ground pepper	to taste
1½ lb	halibut fillets	750 g
24	shrimps or prawns, shell on	24
24	clams in the shell	24
24	mussels in the shell	24
1½ lb	crab in the shell	750 g
for garnish	minced green onions	for garnish
for garnish	minced fresh basil	for garnish

METHOD — continued

napkins. Remind your friends and family not to wear silk—this is a messy meal.

In a large, preferably shallow pan, bring the sauce to a boil. Add the cubed halibut, then cover and reduce the heat. Three minutes later, check to see if the fish is about half done; if it is, add the shrimp or prawns for about 3 minutes, then add the clams, and 2 minutes later add the mussels and crab. Be sure to put the lid back on after each addition, and don't let the temperature drop too low—return briefly to a boil each time you add to the pot. Don't overcook!

Ladle into the heated bowls, evenly distributing the various types of seafood. Garnish with green onions and basil. Serve hot with lots of bread and wine.

I love the dense texture of halibut. You need to pay attention when you're cooking this; if you overcook halibut, the flaky quality disappears and the fish becomes cottony and flavorless. Cooking it with the skin on helps keep it moist. Serves 4

SAFFRON & CHORIZO HALIBUT BOULANGÈRE

INGREDIENTS

2 lb	chicken bones	1kg
1	carrot, cut in two	1
1	onion, quartered	1
4	whole cloves garlic	4
13–15	slices chorizo sausage	13–15
1	bouquet garni, recipe follows	1
to taste	salt and pepper	to taste
2 Tbsp	vegetable oil	30 mL
2	onions, sliced as thinly as possible	2
4	Yukon Gold potatoes, peeled, washed, and cut into ¼-inch (6-mm) slices	4
12	saffron strands	12
4	½-lb (250-g) halibut fillets, with skin	4
2 Tbsp	Parmesan cheese, grated	30 mL

continues on next page

METHOD

Place the bones in a large pot. Add water to cover along with the carrot, quartered onion, garlic, chorizo slices, and bouquet garni. Season with salt and pepper. Bring the stock to a boil and simmer for 20 to 25 minutes, regularly skimming the scum off the surface. Remove the stock from the heat. Set the sausages aside, and discard the chicken bones, vegetables, and bouquet garni.

In a medium pot, heat the oil over low heat and sweat the sliced onions for 15 minutes without letting them color. Stir often to prevent the onions from sticking. Season with salt and pepper. Increase the heat to medium. Add the potato slices to the onions, cover with the chicken stock, and simmer for 15 minutes. Increase the heat to high. Bring the stock to a boil, add the saffron strands, and cook for 5 to 6 minutes. Remove from the heat.

Bouquet Garni

5–6	fresh parsley stems, no leaves	5–6
2	sprigs fresh thyme	2
1	bay leaf	1

Preheat the oven to 425°F (220°C). In a 12-inch (3.5-L) ovenproof ceramic dish, place a row of sliced potatoes, then the chorizo slices. Place the halibut pieces on top and top with the remaining potatoes. Add enough cooking liquid to just cover the fish and potatoes. Sprinkle with Parmesan cheese, season with salt and pepper, and bake for 10 to 15 minutes. Serve from the baking dish.

Bouquet Garni

With kitchen string, tie together the parsley stems, thyme, and bay leaf. You can also tie them up in cheesecloth for easy removal.

A good fish stew has three basic parts: the flavor base, the broth, and the fish. Each is easy to master. This one highlights many of the bright flavors of the Mediterranean. Some would call it a bouillabaisse, but that makes it sound fancy and difficult. It's just a fish stew that tastes so good you'll forget what it's called anyway!

You can buy the fish bones from your local fishmonger. Serves 4–6

MEDITERRANEAN HALIBUT STEW

INGREDIENTS

2 lb	bones from white fish such as halibut, snapper, and cod	1 kg
splash	olive oil	splash
1	fennel bulb, chopped (discard the stringy stalks and woody core)	1
2	onions, chopped	2
4	cloves garlic, sliced	4
1 tsp	fennel seeds	5 mL
1 cup	white wine	250 mL
1	28-oz (796-mL) can ripe tomatoes, chopped or puréed	1
pinch	hot pepper flakes	pinch
2 pinches	saffron threads	2 pinches
2–3	bay leaves	2–3
pinch	salt	pinch
1	orange, zest and juice	1
1½ lb	halibut, cut into large chunks	750 g

METHOD

To make the fish broth, cover the fish bones with 4 to 5 cups (1 to 1.25 L) of water and simmer for 20 minutes. Skim off and discard as much of the foam that rises to the surface as possible; it makes the broth murky. Strain and reserve the broth.

Splash some olive oil into a soup pot over medium-high heat. Sauté the fennel, onions, garlic, and fennel seeds until they soften (about 5 minutes). Pour in the wine and simmer for another 5 minutes.

Add the tomatoes, hot pepper flakes, saffron, bay leaves, reserved fish stock, and salt. Simmer for 20 minutes or so, just long enough for the flavors to brighten but not long enough for them to begin to dull.

At the last minute, zest the orange into the stew and squeeze in the juice. Gently stir in the fish and simmer for another few minutes until it cooks through. Ladle away and enjoy!

For years I'd go to my favorite Indian restaurant, the Curry Pot (now closed), and order this dish. I just couldn't bring myself to order anything else because it was so darned delicious. I was delighted when I was able to re-create this fond memory at home. Look for the coconut cream powder at stores that specialize in Indian food. It's a great way to thicken sauces as well as flavor them with the nutty, compelling taste of coconut. Serves 4

HALIBUT IN A COCONUT SAUCE

INGREDIENTS

3 Tbsp	olive oil	45 mL
1	medium onion, finely chopped	1
3	cloves garlic, minced	3
1	medium tomato, chopped	1
1	1-inch (2.5-cm) piece fresh ginger	1
2 Tbsp	hot pepper flakes	30 mL
1 Tbsp	salt	15 mL
1 Tbsp	ground cumin	15 mL
1 Tbsp	ground coriander	15 mL
1 Tbsp	turmeric	15 mL
4 oz	coconut cream powder	100 g
½ cup	water	125 mL
4	6-oz (170-g) halibut fillets	4
1 cup	yogurt or whipping cream	250 mL

METHOD

Heat the oil in a frying pan over medium-high heat. Sauté the onion and garlic until they're soft and semi-transparent, about 15 minutes. Add the tomato, ginger, hot pepper flakes, salt, cumin, coriander, and turmeric. Cook for about 10 minutes.

Mix the coconut cream powder with the water and add it to the pan. Add more water if needed to thin the sauce. Add the halibut pieces and gently simmer until flaky, about 15 minutes. Add the yogurt or whipping cream and cook for about 5 minutes. (If using yogurt, be sure the mixture doesn't come to a boil, as the sauce will curdle.) Serve immediately.

The spice paste and marinade can be made several days ahead and refrigerated. Serves 6

HALIBUT & PRAWNS
IN LEMON GRASS COCONUT CURRY SAUCE

INGREDIENTS

Spice Paste

4	dried chilies, chopped	4
1	small onion, chopped	1
2	cloves garlic	2
4	stalks lemon grass, thinly sliced	4
1 tsp	shrimp paste	5 mL

Marinade

½ cup	coconut milk	125 mL
1 Tbsp	curry powder	15 mL
2 Tbsp	white sugar	30 mL
1 tsp	salt	5 mL
1 tsp	fish sauce	5 mL

continues on next page

METHOD

Process all the Spice Paste ingredients in a food processor until smooth. Set aside.

Mix together all the marinade ingredients. Cover the halibut and prawns with the marinade and place in the refrigerator for 15 minutes.

Heat the oil in a wok over high heat. Fry the Spice Paste for 30 seconds. Add ½ cup (125 mL) of the coconut milk and the lemon grass and bring to a boil. Lower the heat and simmer for 5 minutes. Remove the lemon grass. Add the marinated fish and prawns, the lime juice, and tamarind water. Cook the fish and prawns for about 1 minute. Add the rest of the coconut milk and simmer for 5 minutes. Add water if desired to thin the sauce.

Halibut & Prawns in Curry Sauce

2 lb	halibut fillets, cubed	1 kg
1 lb	tiger prawns, shelled	500 g
1 Tbsp	oil	15 mL
1½ cups	coconut milk, divided	375 mL
2	stalks lemon grass, lightly pounded	2
¼ cup	lime juice	60 mL
½ cup	tamarind water	125 mL

I learned to make this recipe at a cooking class in Phuket, Thailand. You can sometimes find small Thai eggplants in Asian markets. They're delicious. Otherwise, stick to the small Japanese eggplants (use 2). They're sweeter than the larger variety. Serves 6–8

THAI GREEN CURRY HALIBUT

INGREDIENTS

4 cups	coconut milk, divided	1 L
1½ oz	Thai green curry paste	30 g
6	small Thai eggplants, cubed	6
2¼ Tbsp	fish sauce	45 mL
2 tsp	palm sugar	10 mL
2	kaffir lime leaves	2
3 lb	halibut, cut into chunks	1.5 kg
1 Tbsp	sweet basil leaves	15 mL

METHOD

Combine one cup of the coconut milk and the green curry paste. Cook down the mixture until the milk starts to separate. Add the remaining coconut milk, eggplants, fish sauce, palm sugar, and lime leaves. Cook until thickened. Add the halibut and basil and cook for 3 to 5 minutes more. Serve with fragrant jasmine rice.

A fish chili may seem a little odd, but it's really tasty and a cooking class hit. Serves 6

WHITE HALIBUT CHILI

INGREDIENTS

1 lb	navy beans, rinsed and drained	500 g
1 Tbsp	extra virgin olive oil	15 mL
1 cup	diced onions	250 mL
4	cloves garlic, minced	4
2	jalapeño peppers, minced	2
2 tsp	whole cumin seeds	10 mL
1½ tsp	dried oregano	7 mL
¼ tsp	cayenne pepper	1 mL
5 cups	chicken stock	1.25 L
1 lb	boneless, skinless halibut, cut into bite-sized pieces	500 g
2 cups	shredded aged cheddar	500 mL
to taste	sea salt and freshly ground black pepper	to taste
2 Tbsp	coarsely chopped cilantro	30 mL
	sour cream and salsa (optional)	

METHOD

Place the beans in a heavy, large pot. Add enough cold water to cover the beans at least 3 inches, and soak overnight. Drain the beans into a colander. In the same pot, heat the oil over medium heat. Add the onions, garlic, jalapeño peppers, cumin, oregano, and cayenne pepper. Add the beans and the chicken stock. Reduce the heat and simmer for 2 hours, or until the beans are tender, adding more stock or water if the mixture looks too dry. Add the halibut and cook over medium heat until the halibut can be flaked apart with a fork, about 10 minutes. When the fish is done, stir in the cheese until it melts. Season to taste with salt and pepper. Sprinkle each serving with cilantro, and serve with the sour cream and salsa, if desired.

PAN ROASTING, SAUTÉING
& FRYING

As migratory carnivores, halibut will eat
almost anything that comes their way as long
as it fits in their mouth: cod, turbot and pollock,
octopus, lamprey, crab, and shrimp provide an
abundant buffet for halibut. They will occasionally
feed on fish closer to the surface, such as
sand lance and herring.

෴

Halibut have few predators: the sea lion,
orca whale, salmon shark,
and man.

෴

Serve this with warm green beans topped with some crisp, crumbled pancetta. Serves 6

PAN-ROASTED HALIBUT
WITH SHALLOT VINAIGRETTE

INGREDIENTS

2 Tbsp	lemon juice	30 mL
1 Tbsp	sherry vinegar	15 mL
½ tsp	Dijon mustard	2 mL
⅔ cup	extra virgin olive oil	150 mL
2 Tbsp	minced shallots	30 mL
2 Tbsp	minced fresh chives	30 mL
to taste	kosher salt	to taste
1 Tbsp	butter	15 mL
1 Tbsp	extra virgin olive oil	15 mL
6	4-oz (100-g) halibut fillets	6
to taste	kosher salt and freshly ground black pepper	to taste

METHOD

To make the vinaigrette, combine the lemon juice, vinegar, mustard, ⅔ cup (150 mL) olive oil, shallots, and chives. Season with salt.

In a large sauté pan, heat the butter and the 1 Tbsp (15 mL) olive oil over high heat. Season the fish fillets with salt and pepper and place in the pan, skin side down. Reduce the heat to medium and cook for 3 to 4 minutes on each side, until cooked through and opaque. Place on serving plates, spoon the vinaigrette over the fillets, and serve immediately.

This is a great dish for the spring and summer when halibut is in season. Look for fresh halibut that's firm and opaque. Avoid halibut that looks very white, as though it's cooked. It isn't as firm in texture and will fall apart easily when cooked. Serves 4

PAN-ROASTED HALIBUT
WITH A CITRUS MUSTARD SEED CRUST
& ROASTED RED PEPPER VINAIGRETTE

INGREDIENTS

3 Tbsp	fine bread crumbs	45 mL
3 Tbsp	yellow mustard seeds	45 mL
3 Tbsp	black mustard seeds	45 mL
3	lemons, zest only, finely chopped	3
1½ tsp	finely chopped fresh parsley	7 mL
¼ tsp	sea salt	1 mL
¼ tsp	freshly ground black pepper	1 mL
2 Tbsp	clarified butter	30 mL
4	7-oz (200-g) halibut fillets	4

continues on next page

METHOD

Preheat the oven to 400°F (200°C). To make the crust mixture, combine the bread crumbs, mustard seeds, lemon zest, parsley, salt, and pepper. Heat the clarified butter in an ovenproof non-stick skillet. Dredge one side of each piece of halibut in the crust mixture. Place in the hot pan with the crust side down. Sear for about 1 minute. Carefully turn the fillets over and transfer the pan to the oven. Bake for about 10 minutes, or until firm to the touch. Serve crust side up on warm plates. Drizzle the vinaigrette over top.

ROASTING PEPPERS

Peppers take on a new personality when roasted. The flavor is smoother and more defined, and the soft flesh is easy to blend into soups, sauces, mayonnaise, vinaigrettes, or whatever you wish. To roast peppers, toss them in a bowl with a little olive oil, salt, and pepper. Char them over a very hot fire, turning them occasionally, until the skins are black all over. (Alternatively, you can roast them in a pan in a 450°F/230°C oven for 30 to 40 minutes, until soft.) Remove them from the heat, put them back into the bowl, and cover them tightly with plastic wrap. When they're cool enough to handle, scrape off the charred skins under cold running water. Remove the core and seeds, leaving the soft roasted pepper flesh.

INGREDIENTS — continued

Roasted Red Pepper Vinaigrette
Makes 1 cup (250 mL)

2	roasted red peppers (see page 17)	2
1	chipotle pepper	1
3 Tbsp	lime juice	45 mL
1 Tbsp	liquid honey	15 mL
1 tsp	minced garlic	5 mL
to taste	sea salt and freshly ground black pepper	to taste
¾ cup	extra virgin olive oil	175 mL

METHOD — continued

Roasted Red Pepper Vinaigrette

Place the red pepper, chipotle pepper, lime juice, honey, garlic, salt, and pepper in a blender. With the motor running, slowly add the olive oil until it's all incorporated. (To make it by hand, finely chop the roasted red peppers and place them in a bowl with the chipotle, lime juice, honey, and garlic. Very slowly add the olive oil, whisking until it's all incorporated.) Season with salt and pepper. This will keep for up to 2 days, covered and refrigerated.

It's become popular to serve lentils with salmon, but they're a real treat served with halibut. Serves 6

PAN-ROASTED HALIBUT
WITH LENTIL & TOMATO VINAIGRETTE

INGREDIENTS

1 cup	French lentils, washed and drained	250 mL
1	small onion studded with a clove	1
1	1-inch (2.5-cm) piece cinnamon stick	1
1	2-inch (5-cm) piece carrot, peeled	1
1	2-inch (5-cm) piece celery	1
1	medium clove garlic, minced	1
½ tsp	sea salt	2 mL
2 Tbsp	balsamic vinegar	30 mL
4 Tbsp	extra virgin olive oil	60 mL
to taste	freshly ground black pepper	to taste
6	5- to 6-oz (150- to 175-g) skinless halibut fillets	6
to taste	sea salt and freshly ground black pepper	to taste
1 Tbsp	vegetable oil	15 mL
2	medium, ripe tomatoes, seeded and finely diced	2
1 Tbsp	finely chopped parsley	15 mL

METHOD

Place the lentils in a pot, and cover with 4 inches (10 cm) of water. Bring to a boil then reduce to a simmer, and skim off any foam. Add the onion, cinnamon stick, carrot, and celery. Simmer until the lentils are tender but not mushy, about 45 minutes. Drain and discard the vegetables and cinnamon stick.

While waiting for the lentils to cook, mash the garlic to a paste with the salt. Whisk in the balsamic vinegar, then slowly beat in the olive oil. Season with pepper. Combine the warm lentils with the vinaigrette and stir well to coat.

Preheat the oven to 350°F (180°C). Season the halibut to taste with salt and pepper. Heat the vegetable oil on medium-high heat in a heavy, ovenproof frying pan. Fry the halibut until golden brown on one side. Flip the fillets over and bake in the oven for 10 minutes.

Mix the tomatoes and parsley into the lentils and spoon onto 6 heated plates. Place the halibut on top of the lentils and serve.

You can use asparagus instead of beans for this handsome hot-weather dish. The halibut may be grilled if you don't want to turn on the oven. Serves 4

PAN-ROASTED HALIBUT
WITH WARM BEAN & TOMATO SALAD

INGREDIENTS

½ lb	green beans, trimmed	250 g
½ lb	yellow beans, trimmed	250 g
1 Tbsp	extra virgin olive oil	15 mL
4	6-oz (175-g) halibut fillets	4
to taste	sea salt and freshly ground black pepper	to taste
4 tsp	balsamic vinegar	20 mL
1½ tsp	sugar	7 mL
½ cup	red onion, thinly sliced	125 mL
3	ripe plum tomatoes, cut into ½-inch (1-cm) cubes	3
3 Tbsp	fresh basil, coarsely chopped	45 mL

METHOD

Bring a large pot of water to a boil and salt liberally. Add the beans and cook until they're tender-crisp, 3 to 5 minutes. Drain and cool under cold water. Pat dry.

Preheat the oven to 400°F (200°C). In a heavy ovenproof frying pan, heat the olive oil over high heat. Season the halibut fillets with salt and pepper and cook in the hot oil for about 3 minutes, until the bottom is browned. Place the pan in the oven and cook the fish until just opaque, about 8 minutes. Place the fish on a heated plate. Cover and keep warm.

Add the beans to the frying pan and sauté over medium heat until the beans are heated through. Add the balsamic vinegar and sugar and stir to combine. Stir in the onion, tomatoes, and basil. Season with salt and pepper. Spoon the bean and tomato mixture around the halibut fillets and serve immediately.

All the flavors of bouillabaisse but easier to prepare! Try this alongside some thick rounds of steamed baby potatoes, tiny green beans, and batons of carrots or yellow beets. Serves 8

PACIFIC HALIBUT

WITH SAFFRON LEEK SAUCE & LEMON AÏOLI

INGREDIENTS

Aïoli

2	fresh, large egg yolks	2
3	large cloves garlic, peeled	3
1 tsp	dry mustard	5 mL
¼ tsp	salt	1 mL
1 cup	quality olive oil	250 mL
2 Tbsp	lemon juice	30 mL
1 Tbsp	minced lemon zest	15 mL

Saffron Leek Sauce

2 Tbsp	olive oil	30 mL
1	medium white onion, chopped	1
2	large leeks, white part only, halved and sliced	2
3	cloves garlic, peeled and minced	3
½ cup	dry white wine	125 mL
1	small dried hot chili, crumbled	1
1 cup	canned Roma tomatoes, puréed	250 mL

continues on next page

METHOD

Aïoli

Combine the egg yolks, garlic, mustard, and salt in a blender or food processor. Blend until the garlic is finely minced. With the machine running, slowly add the oil through the feed tube until the aïoli begins to emulsify and thicken. Add the lemon juice and blend quickly to combine. Fold in the lemon zest. Refrigerate in a covered container for up to 3 days.

Saffron Leek Sauce

Heat the olive oil in a sauté pan over medium-low heat and cook the onion and leek until very soft and translucent. Add the garlic, wine, and chili. Increase the heat and simmer for 3 minutes. Stir in the tomato purée, fennel seed, and herb bundle. Crumble the saffron into the fish stock or clam juice and let stand for 5 minutes, then add to the sauce. Simmer, uncovered, for 20 minutes. Remove the herb bundle and discard. Combine the

pinch	fennel seed	pinch
1	herb bundle (strip orange zest, sprig rosemary, and sprig thyme, wrapped in 3-inch/8-cm piece of leek leaf and tied together with string	1
½ tsp	lightly crushed saffron threads	2 mL
1½ cups	warm fish stock (see page 176) or bottled clam juice	375 mL
1 tsp	balsamic vinegar	5 mL
1 Tbsp	cornstarch	15 mL
to taste	salt and freshly ground black pepper	to taste

Halibut

3 Tbsp	canola or peanut oil	45 mL
8	4-oz (100-g) halibut fillets, at least 1 inch (2.5 cm) thick, skin on	8
to taste	salt and freshly ground black pepper	to taste
¼ cup	cornstarch	60 mL
to taste	cayenne pepper	to taste

vinegar and cornstarch to make a paste and whisk into the sauce. Simmer to thicken nicely. Season with salt and pepper. Keep the sauce warm.

Halibut

Preheat the oven to 400°F (200°C). Heat the oil in a large ovenproof non-stick pan over medium-high heat. Season the fish with salt and pepper and dip the flesh side into cornstarch to coat, shaking off any excess. Sauté the halibut, flesh side down, over medium-high heat for 2 minutes, or until crisp and golden on one side. Turn the fish over and place the pan immediately into the oven to finish cooking, about 5 to 8 minutes, depending on the thickness of the fillets. Be careful not to overcook the halibut as it's a lean fish and can dry out quickly.

Serve the fish in a pool of sauce, topped with the Saffron Leek Sauce, a generous dollop of aïoli, and a dusting of cayenne.

This recipe is beautiful in its simplicity. A perfectly moist roasted halibut steak perches on top of a light cloud of sweet potato purée. The acidity of the pickled onions is the perfect complement to balance the culinary harmony. Serves 6

PAN-ROASTED HALIBUT
WITH SWEET POTATO PURÉE & PICKLED ONIONS

INGREDIENTS

Pickled Onion

1	red onion, sliced into ½-inch (1-cm) rings	1
½ cup	red wine	125 mL
½ cup	red wine vinegar	125 mL
1	clove garlic, minced	1
1 tsp	mustard seed, toasted	5 mL
1 tsp	fennel seed, toasted	5 mL
2 tsp	kosher salt	10 mL
1	bay leaf	1

Sweet Potato Purée

1	large sweet potato, halved horizontally	1
1 Tbsp	unsalted butter	15 mL
1 Tbsp	white truffle oil	15 mL
to taste	kosher salt and white pepper	to taste

continues on next page

METHOD

Pickled Onion

Combine all the ingredients and refrigerate for 24 hours (place a weight on the onions so they're fully submerged).

Sweet Potato Purée

Place the sweet potatoes, skin side down, in an oven-proof dish or tray and bake for 30 minutes. Turn the potatoes and bake for a further 20 minutes, or until easily pierced with a fork.

Remove the potatoes and, when they're cool enough to handle, scoop out the flesh and mix with the butter, truffle oil, salt, and pepper. Stir until the butter has completely melted into the mixture and set aside.

Halibut

1 Tbsp	olive oil	15 mL
1 Tbsp	unsalted butter	15 mL
1½ lb	fresh halibut fillet, cut into 6 pieces	750 g
to taste	kosher salt and white pepper	to taste

Halibut

Preheat a medium frying pan over moderately high heat. Heat the olive oil and butter, but not to the point of smoking. Season the fish with salt and pepper and add it to the pan, flesh side down. Cook the fish for 5 minutes, then turn it and cook the other side for a further 4 minutes.

To Serve

Arrange the sweet potato purée in the center of warmed dinner plates. Place the fish on the purée, arrange the pickled onions around the fish, and serve.

With only a few ingredients, the success lies in the quality of the beef stock. Make sure it's flavorful and rich.
Serves 4

PAN-SEARED HALIBUT
WITH BEEF STOCK

INGREDIENTS

4	6-oz (175-g) halibut fillets	4
to taste	sea salt and freshly ground black pepper	to taste
½ cup	all-purpose flour	125 mL
½ tsp	paprika	2 mL
2 Tbsp	vegetable oil	30 mL
2 cups	high quality beef stock	500 mL

METHOD

Preheat the oven to 400°F (200°C). Season the halibut with salt and pepper. Mix the flour and paprika together on a plate.

Heat the oil over medium heat in a large, heavy frying pan. Dip both sides of the halibut into the flour mixture. Fry on both sides until golden brown. Transfer to a baking pan and bake for 5 to 7 minutes, until the flesh turns opaque in the middle.

While the halibut bakes, pour off all the oil from the frying pan. Add the beef stock and bring to a boil, scraping up any bits clinging to the frying pan. Reduce the beef stock by half. Season with salt and pepper. Remove from the heat, strain through a sieve, and keep warm.

Place the halibut on heated plates. Pour the beef stock over top and serve immediately.

Nothing beats the flavor of fresh halibut in season. Make the salsa the night before—the flavor will be even better. For a really quick meal, spread a commercial salsa on the fillet and bake. Serves 4

HALIBUT

WITH MANGO & RED PEPPER SALSA

INGREDIENTS

1	mango, peeled and diced	1
1	red bell pepper, diced	1
¼ cup	chopped white onion	60 mL
1 Tbsp	fresh cilantro	15 mL
1	lime, juice of	1
1 lb	halibut fillets	500 g
¼ cup	flour	60 mL
¼ tsp	salt	1 mL
1 Tbsp	canola oil	15 mL

METHOD

Combine the mango, red pepper, onion, cilantro, and lime juice. Allow the mixture to sit for at least half an hour to allow the flavors to mingle.

Cut the halibut into 4 pieces. Combine the flour and salt in a plastic bag. Add the halibut pieces one at a time and shake the bag to coat the fish with flour. Heat the oil over medium heat in a non-stick frying pan. Add the halibut and fry until the fish is cooked and lightly browned on both sides, about 6 minutes for each side. The fish should be opaque and flake easily when pierced with a fork. Serve the halibut topped with plenty of salsa.

Jasmine rice and stir-fried red peppers and snow peas will round out this meal. Serves 6

PAN-SEARED HALIBUT
WITH BURNT ORANGE & WASABI GLAZE

INGREDIENTS

6	6-oz (175-g) halibut fillets	6
to taste	sea salt and freshly ground black pepper	to taste
1 Tbsp	vegetable oil	15 mL

Burnt Orange & Wasabi Glaze

¾ cup	granulated sugar	175 mL
¼ cup	water	60 mL
½ cup	red wine	125 mL
¼ tsp	sea salt	1 mL
1	orange, juice and grated rind	1
1 Tbsp	prepared wasabi	15 mL
4 Tbsp	unsalted butter	60 mL
2	green onions, chopped	2

METHOD

Preheat the oven to 350ºF (180ºC). Season the halibut with salt and pepper. Heat the oil in a heavy frying pan over medium-high heat and cook the halibut until it's lightly browned on both sides. Bake in the oven for 8 to 10 minutes, until opaque throughout. Place on heated plates or a platter. Spoon the glaze over the halibut and serve immediately.

Burnt Orange & Wasabi Glaze

To make the glaze, combine the sugar and water in a small, heavy saucepan. Cook over high heat without stirring until the sugar turns a dark mahogany brown. Watch the caramel carefully. You'll see the bubbles rise more rapidly and become looser and less viscous. Have a sieve on hand that covers the pot completely.

Remove from the heat, stand back, and immediately pour the red wine through the sieve, into the pot. The caramel will splutter furiously. The sieve will protect you from burns.

When the spluttering stops, transfer the caramel to a bowl and add the salt. Cool completely and add the orange juice and rind. (The glaze may be made to this point up to 4 weeks in advance.) Cover and refrigerate.

Just before serving, bring the glaze to a boil. Whisk in the wasabi. Remove from the heat and whisk in the butter, 1 Tbsp (15 mL) at a time. Add the green onions.

Halibut's mild flavor is nicely complemented by the savory relish. You can also toss some of the relish with salad greens and serve the fish over top with the rest of the relish as garnish. The relish can be made earlier in the day, refrigerated and brought up to room temperature before serving. If you do this, add the feta cheese and avocado just before serving so that they don't break down. Serves 4

PAN-SEARED HALIBUT

WITH MEDITERRANEAN RELISH

INGREDIENTS

Relish

½	avocado	½
3 Tbsp	extra virgin olive oil	45 mL
1½ Tbsp	lemon juice, freshly squeezed	22 mL
2 Tbsp	English cucumber, seeded and cut into ¼ inch (6 cm) dice	30 mL
2 Tbsp	red bell pepper, seeded and cut into ¼ inch (6 cm) dice	30 mL
2 Tbsp	yellow bell pepper, seeded and cut into ¼ inch (6 cm) dice	30 mL
3 Tbsp	crumbled feta cheese	45 mL
1	Roma tomato, cut into ¼ inch (6 cm) dice	1
¼	red onion, cut into a fine julienne	¼
2 Tbsp	sliced, pitted black olives	30 mL
1 tsp	salt	5 mL
2 tsp	freshly ground black pepper	10 mL

continues on next page

METHOD

Relish

Place the avocado in a medium bowl. Pour in the oil and lemon juice. Add the cucumber, red and yellow peppers, feta cheese, tomato, onion, and olives. Gently combine the ingredients and season with salt and pepper.

Marinade

Combine the marinade ingredients in a small bowl and mix well.

Halibut

Place the halibut in a shallow glass dish. Pour the marinade over the fish, turning several times so the fillets are well coated. Refrigerate and marinate for 2 to 4 hours.

Remove the fish from the marinade. Heat the oil in a large sauté pan over medium-high heat. When the oil is hot, sauté the halibut for 3 minutes on one side.

Marinade

¼ cup	canola oil	60 mL
1	clove garlic, minced	1
1 Tbsp	finely chopped fresh basil	15 mL
2 Tbsp	white wine	30 mL
1 Tbsp	freshly squeezed lemon juice	15 mL
½ tsp	freshly ground black pepper	2 mL

Halibut

4	8-oz (225-g) halibut fillets, ¾ inch (2 cm) thick	4
3 Tbsp	canola oil	45 mL

Turn the heat to medium and sauté the other side for 2 minutes more, or until the fish is flaky in the middle.

To serve, place each portion of halibut in the center of a large plate. Spoon the relish over the halibut and serve immediately.

A quick-cooking dish with minimal ingredients that accent the fine flavor of halibut, rather than mask it. If fresh chives aren't available, replace with 1 finely chopped green onion. For a different lemon/herb taste, use 1 Tbsp (15 mL) of chopped fresh tarragon, oregano, or basil. Serves 2

PAN-FRIED HALIBUT
WITH LEMON CHIVE BUTTER

INGREDIENTS

2 Tbsp	olive oil	30 mL
2	5-oz (150-g) halibut fillets	2
to taste	salt and white pepper	to taste
2 Tbsp	melted butter	30 mL
½	lemon, juice of	½
1 Tbsp	chopped fresh chives	15 mL

METHOD

Put the olive oil in a non-stick skillet over medium-high heat. Season the halibut with salt and pepper and cook for 3 to 4 minutes per side (a little longer if the fillets are thick), or until cooked through. Divide the fish between 2 heated dinner plates.

Drain the oil from the pan, then add the butter, lemon juice, and chives. Cook and stir until the butter just melts. Pour the butter over the fish and serve.

This is a stunning way to serve halibut for a special treat. I first made this dish for my friend Don Harron, and it remains a memorable meal for me! For this recipe, fillets are preferable to steaks. If fresh halibut is in season, treat yourself to a thick center cut. To cut back on the fat, serve the sauce on the side. Serves 6

FRESH HALIBUT
WITH BASIL & PARSLEY SAUCE

INGREDIENTS

½ cup	white wine	125 mL
¼ cup	lemon juice	60 mL
1 cup	whipping cream	250 mL
¼ cup	chopped fresh parsley	60 mL
¼ cup	finely chopped fresh basil	60 mL
1 Tbsp	capers	15 mL
½ cup	flour	125 mL
to taste	salt and freshly ground pepper	to taste
½ cup	butter	125 mL
2 lb	halibut fillets	1 kg

METHOD

Combine the white wine and lemon juice in a medium saucepan and cook for 2 to 3 minutes. Add the whipping cream and cook until the liquid is reduced by half to about ¾ cup (175 mL). Add the parsley, basil, and capers and whisk until well blended. Season to taste with salt and pepper. Set aside.

Season the flour with salt and pepper. Dredge the fish lightly in the seasoned flour.

In a large skillet, heat the butter, add the fish, and fry on high heat until the fish just starts to flake. The trick is not to overcook it. Keep testing. Reheat the sauce, pour it over fish, and serve immediately.

This is a delicious fish dish to create quickly when the mood strikes. Serve it with basmati rice or baby potatoes on the side. Serves 2

HALIBUT

WITH SQUASH RIBBONS & LEMON BUTTER SAUCE

INGREDIENTS

1	lemon, zest and juice	1
¾ lb	boneless halibut fillet, skin removed, cut across the grain on a diagonal, into 1-inch (2.5-cm) thick slices	375 g
to taste	salt and cayenne pepper	to taste
¼ cup	all-purpose flour	60 mL
2–3 Tbsp	olive oil	30–45 mL
1	clove garlic, minced	1
½ cup	white wine	125 mL
2 Tbsp	butter, cold	30 mL
1 Tbsp	minced fresh parsley	15 mL

Zucchini Ribbons

2	small 6-inch (15-cm) zucchini	2
1 Tbsp	unsalted butter	15 mL
to taste	salt	to taste

METHOD

Scrub the lemon well. Using a microplane grater, remove the zest from the lemon. Set aside.

Cut the lemon in half, remove the seeds, and use a citrus reamer to remove the juice. You should have about 3 to 4 Tbsp (45 to 60 mL). Set aside. To make the zucchini ribbons, wash the zucchini and remove the ends, but don't peel. Using a vegetable peeler, slice the zucchini, lengthwise, into paper-thin ribbons.

To cook the zucchini, in a separate pan, heat the butter over medium-high heat and add the zucchini ribbons. Sauté until the ribbons are just tender. Season with salt and keep warm.

Season fish slices with salt and cayenne. Place the flour on another plate and thoroughly dredge both sides of the fish slices to coat.

Heat the olive oil in a non-stick sauté pan over medium-high heat and sauté the fish for 1 to 2 minutes per side or until golden. Remove the fish from the pan. Pile the warm zucchini ribbons into the centre of two warm serving plates and arrange the fish slices overtop.

Add the garlic, white wine, lemon zest, and juice to the fish pan. Bring to a boil over high heat, scraping up any browned bits, and simmer for 3 minutes, or until the liquid is reduced to ¼ cup (60 mL). Remove the pan from the heat and whisk in the cold butter. Pour the hot sauce over the fish and zucchini, sprinkle with parsley, and serve immediately with steamed potatoes or rice.

Halibut cheeks are undeniably my favorite part of the fish. The approach of spring brings these fabulous cheeks to market. They're moist and succulent and can be interchanged with any fish in your favorite fish recipes. I urge you to try them. If fish were addictive, then cheeks would do it. Serves 6

WEST COAST HALIBUT CHEEKS

INGREDIENTS

2½ lb	fresh halibut cheeks	1.125 kg
⅓ cup	unbleached all-purpose flour	75 mL
2 Tbsp	extra virgin olive oil	30 mL
2 Tbsp	unsalted butter	30 mL
3	shallots, finely minced	3
3 Tbsp	flat-leaf parsley, chopped	45 mL
1 Tbsp	capers	15 mL
2 tsp	chopped fresh thyme	10 mL
⅔ cup	white wine	150 mL
to taste	sea salt	to taste
to taste	freshly ground white pepper	to taste

METHOD

Dredge the halibut cheeks in the flour, tapping off the excess. Heat the oil and butter together in a frying pan, add the halibut cheeks, and cook until golden-brown, about 2 to 3 minutes per side. Add the shallots, parsley, capers, and thyme. Continue to cook for 4 more minutes.

Add the wine to the pan along with the salt and white pepper and cook until the cheeks are cooked through. Depending on the size of the cheeks, this may be another minute or so. Serve the cheeks with steamed baby potatoes or your favorite vegetable, and ladle the pan juices over top.

Have all the ingredients chopped and ready to go before whipping up this quick stir-fry. For a sweeter, less salty taste use hoisin sauce instead of oyster sauce. For a spicy stir-fry, add Asian-style hot chili sauce when adding the oyster sauce. Serves 4

SIZZLING HALIBUT & SEAFOOD STIR-FRY

INGREDIENTS

¼ cup	oyster sauce	60 mL
2 Tbsp	light soy sauce	30 mL
1 tsp	honey	5 mL
2 tsp	sesame oil	10 mL
1 Tbsp	rice vinegar	15 mL
2	green onions, finely chopped	2
2 Tbsp	vegetable oil	30 mL
2	cloves garlic, finely chopped	2
2 tsp	chopped fresh ginger	10 mL
8	medium to large shrimp, peeled and cut in half lengthwise	8
8	large scallops, cut in half lengthwise	8
½ lb	halibut fillets, cubed	250 g
4	heads baby bok choy, trimmed and separated into leaves	4
1	medium yellow or red bell pepper, cut into small cubes	1
to taste	freshly ground black pepper	to taste

METHOD

In a bowl, combine the oyster sauce, soy sauce, honey, sesame oil, rice vinegar, and green onions.

Heat the vegetable oil in a wok or large skillet over medium-high heat. Add the garlic and ginger and stir-fry for 30 seconds. Add the shrimp, scallops, and halibut and cook for 3 to 4 minutes, or until just cooked through. Transfer the seafood to a plate. Add the baby bok choy and bell pepper to the pan and stir-fry for 2 minutes. Add the oyster sauce mixture and ¼ cup (60 mL) of cold water and bring to a simmer. Return the seafood to the pan and cook until just heated through. Season with pepper and serve.

Making great beer batter is simple. Keep the batter as cold as possible and work in small batches. The colder the batter, the bigger the reaction when it hits the hot oil, resulting in a lighter, crispier crust. Working with small batches in the fryer helps keep the oil at a consistent temperature, which means the food absorbs less oil. Serves 4

PUBLIC HOUSE FISH 'N' CHIPS

INGREDIENTS

Fish

2 cups	all-purpose flour	500 mL
1 Tbsp	baking powder	15 mL
1 tsp	salt	5 mL
½ tsp	garlic powder	2 mL
1 tsp	white pepper	5 mL
¼ tsp	cayenne pepper	1 mL
1	12-oz (341-mL) bottle dark ale	1
1½ lb	halibut, tilapia, or cod fillets	750 g
1 cup	cornstarch	250 mL

Chips

4	large russet potatoes, sliced and soaked in water	4
12 cups	vegetable oil	3 L

continues on next page

METHOD

To make the batter, combine the flour, baking powder, salt, garlic powder, white pepper, and cayenne pepper in a large bowl. Slowly whisk in the ale until well blended and smooth. Refrigerate until needed.

Preheat the oven to 200°F (95°C). Heat the oil in a large deep pot or Dutch oven to 350°F (180°C). Line a rimmed cookie sheet with newspaper and place a cooling rack on top.

Drain the potatoes, then lay them on paper towel to soak up excess water. Working in small batches, carefully add the sliced potatoes to the pot and cook until soft, but still pale in appearance, for about 8 minutes. Remove the potatoes and drain on a rack placed on top of the prepared cookie sheet. Keep warm in the oven.

Ensure the oil temperature has returned to 350°F (180°C). Lightly dredge the fish in cornstarch and dip in the batter, coating evenly. Working in small batches,

Tartar Sauce

1 cup	mayonnaise	250 mL
2 Tbsp	chopped dill pickle	30 mL
2 Tbsp	fresh lime juice	30 mL
1 Tbsp	Limoncello	15 mL
1 Tbsp	wasabi or horseradish	15 mL
1 tsp	lime zest	5 mL

carefully add the battered fish to the pot and cook until golden, about 6 to 8 minutes, turning once. Remove the fish and drain on the rack placed on top of the prepared cookie sheet. Keep warm in the oven.

Refry the potatoes until golden and crisp, about 3 minutes, then drain on newspaper. Serve with sea salt, malt vinegar, lemon wedges, and tartar sauce.

To make the tartar sauce, combine the tartar sauce ingredients in a medium bowl and refrigerate until ready to serve.

I had this relish in Thailand, served with squid. It goes well with this particular halibut too. Make sure your halibut fillets are on the thin side so that they'll cook through quickly. Serves 4–6

CRISPY HALIBUT
WITH SWEET & SOUR CUCUMBER-BEER RELISH

INGREDIENTS

¼ cup	egg whites	60 mL
¼ tsp	sea salt	1 mL
pinch	freshly ground black pepper	pinch
1 Tbsp	Dijon mustard	15 mL
dash	Tabasco sauce	dash
¼ cup	cornstarch	60 mL
4	4-oz (100-g) halibut fillets	4
6 cups	soft white bread crumbs, made from day old bread, crusts removed	1.5 L
	vegetable oil for frying	

continues on next page

METHOD

Beat together the egg whites, salt, pepper, mustard, Tabasco, and cornstarch. Dip the halibut into the cornstarch mixture, then dredge with the bread crumbs, patting them on firmly with your hands.

Heat ½ inch (1 cm) vegetable oil in a large, heavy frying pan over medium heat. Fry the halibut fillets until golden brown on both sides and cooked through. Serve immediately, with the relish on the side.

Sweet & Sour Cucumber-Beer Relish

Combine the vinegar and sugar in a non-corrodible saucepan. Bring to a boil, and continue boiling for 5 minutes. Remove from the heat and cool.

Toss the sliced cucumbers with the salt. Place in a sieve and weight down with a bowl that fits into the sieve. Allow the cucumbers to drain for an hour. Gently squeeze the cucumbers with your hands to remove any water. Place in a bowl. (The relish may be made to this point

Sweet & Sour Cucumber-Beer Relish

1 cup	white vinegar	250 mL
10 Tbsp	granulated sugar	150 mL
1	English cucumber, sliced paper thin	1
2 tsp	salt	10 mL
½ cup	beer	125 mL
4	shallots, thinly sliced	4

a few hours in advance.) Pour off any liquid that has accumulated around the cucumbers before proceeding.

Just before serving, mix the beer with the vinegar syrup. Pour over the cucumbers and mix gently. Scatter the shallots on top.

Serve a green salad or a pot of basmati rice alongside the halibut. Serves 6

CORNMEAL-COATED HALIBUT
WITH ROASTED PEPPER SALSA

INGREDIENTS

¼ cup	all-purpose flour	60 mL
to taste	salt and pepper	to taste
2	egg whites	2
1 Tbsp	milk or water	15 mL
1 cup	cornmeal	250 mL
1 Tbsp	yellow mustard seed (optional)	15 mL
6	5-oz (150-g) halibut steaks	6
¼ cup	canola oil	60 mL

continues on next page

METHOD

Preheat the oven to 450°F (230°C). Mix the flour, salt, and pepper in a shallow bowl. Whisk together the egg whites and milk in another shallow bowl until they're well combined. Combine the cornmeal, mustard seed (if desired), and salt and spread out onto a plate. Dredge the halibut in the flour mixture, covering all sides, then dip into the egg mixture, coating the halibut completely. Dredge in the cornmeal mixture to coat it on all sides. (You can prepare the fish ahead to this point and refrigerate it on a rack, lightly covered with parchment, but remember to take the chill off before cooking it.)

Preheat a griddle or sauté pan with the canola oil. Check the temperature of the hot pan by cooking a bread cube; if it colors right away, the oil is hot enough. Pan-fry the halibut, turning it once until both sides are nicely browned and crisp. If you don't have a large enough frying pan or flat griddle, cook the fish in

Roasted Red Pepper Salsa
Makes about 1½ cups (375 mL)

2	red bell peppers	2
1	each dried ancho and morita chili	1
1–3 tsp	Chimayo chili powder	5–15 mL
1	orange, juice and zest	1
4	cloves garlic, sliced	4
1	bunch green onions, minced	1
1 Tbsp	minced cilantro	15 mL
1 Tbsp	extra virgin olive oil	15 mL
to taste	salt and freshly ground black pepper	to taste

successive batches. Transfer to a baking sheet or rack and finish it in the oven, about 10 minutes, depending on the thickness of the fish. To check for doneness, poke a little hole with the tip of a paring knife at the thickest point; the center of each steak should be opaque and flaky. Serve with the pepper salsa on the side.

Roasted Red Pepper Salsa

Roast the bell peppers over an open flame until the outer skin is charred on all sides. Pop them into a plastic bag to steam. Put both dried peppers into a small bowl, add enough hot water to cover, cover securely, and microwave for several minutes to soften. When they're soft and cool enough to handle, remove and discard the seeds and chop the peppers finely.

Peel the blackened bell peppers. Don't worry about every little bit of black—a little gives a rustic charm to the finished dish. Remove the seeds and chop the peppers into strips of whatever size you like. Add the chopped chilies, chili powder, orange juice and zest, garlic, green onions, cilantro, olive oil, salt and pepper. Taste and adjust the seasoning if required.

Traditional ginger-fried squid is time-consuming and messy to make at home. With much less work, this halibut variation has similar flavors. Serves 4

HALIBUT IN GINGER-LEMON SAUCE

INGREDIENTS

1 lb	halibut fillets, cut into 4 equal pieces	500 g
2 Tbsp	canola oil, divided	30 mL
1	onion, finely sliced	1
1	carrot, finely julienned	1
2	celery stalks, finely sliced	2
6	cloves garlic, sliced	6
4 Tbsp	grated fresh ginger	60 mL
4 Tbsp	brown sugar	60 mL
1–2	lemons, juice and zest	1–2
2 Tbsp	soy sauce	30 mL
1 tsp	hot chili paste	5 mL
1 cup	vegetable stock or water	250 mL
1 tsp	corn starch dissolved in 1 Tbsp (15 mL) cold water	5 mL
2 Tbsp	minced cilantro	30 mL
3–4	green onions, minced	3–4

METHOD

Pan-steam the fish in 1 Tbsp (15 mL) of the canola oil over low heat in a non-stick pan. Use a lid that fits snugly over the fish in the pan. Turn the fish frequently and reduce the heat if the fish sizzles or browns. After 5 to 7 minutes, or when the fish is flaky and opaque, remove it to a plate and loosely cover to keep warm.

Reheat the pan with the remaining canola oil, and cook the onion until tender and beginning to color. Stir in the carrot, celery, garlic, and ginger and cook until they smell fragrant and the carrot is still crisp. Add the brown sugar, lemon juice and zest, soy sauce, hot chili paste, and stock. Bring to a boil and taste, adjusting the seasoning with lemon juice, soy sauce, and chili paste, if necessary. Stir in the dissolved cornstarch and cook until the sauce is clear. Add the fish. Pour into a serving bowl and garnish with the cilantro and green onions just before serving.

HALIBUT POACHED IN RED WINE | pages 32 – 33

Tony de Luca — *Recipes from Wine Country*

HALIBUT & SEAFOOD HOTPOT WITH SAFFRON AÏOLI | pages 38 – 39

Anna & Michael Olson — *Inn on the Twenty*

SAFFRON & CHORIZO HALIBUT BOULANGÈRE | pages 42 – 43

Alain Rayé — *La Régalade*

You can grill the halibut without the batter instead of deep-frying it. Serves 6

FISH TACOS

INGREDIENTS

¼ cup	each ketchup, mayonnaise, and sour cream	60 mL
to taste	salt and pepper	to taste
1 cup	all-purpose flour	250 mL
1 tsp	sea salt	5 mL
½ tsp	ground pepper	2 mL
1 cup	dark beer, at room temperature	250 mL
1¾ lb	skinless, boneless halibut fillets, cut into about 24 strips	875 g
2	limes, halved	2
	vegetable oil for deep frying	
12	small 7-inch (18-cm) corn or flour tortillas	12
1½ cups	finely shredded cabbage or iceberg lettuce	375 mL
2	large tomatoes, chopped	2
to taste	hot pepper sauce (optional)	to taste

METHOD

In a bowl, stir together the ketchup, mayonnaise, and sour cream. Add the salt and pepper to taste. In another bowl, combine the flour, salt, and pepper. Add the beer; whisk until smooth.

Sprinkle the fish with salt and pepper; squeeze the juice of 1 lime over the strips. Let the batter and fish stand for 15 minutes. Add the fish to the batter.

Preheat the oven to 350°F (180°C). Stack the tortillas, wrap them in foil, and bake for about 5 minutes or until warm. In a medium frying pan or wok, add 1 inch (2.5 cm) of the oil. Attach a deep-fry thermometer to the side. Heat the oil to 350°F (180°C). Slide 4 fish strips into the oil. Fry until golden, about 3 minutes. Transfer to a paper towel. Repeat with the remaining fish.

Fill each tortilla with 2 fish strips. Top with the mayo mixture, cabbage, tomatoes, juice from the remaining lime, and hot pepper sauce.

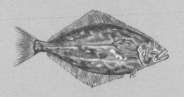

IN THE OVEN

Halibut spawn during the winter months,
the peak occurring from December through February.
Males become sexually mature at 7 or 8 years of age;
females at 8 to 12 years. Depending on their
size, females lay two to three million eggs annually.
Most spawning takes place off the edge of the
continental shelf in deep waters of 200 to 300
fathoms (1,200 to 1,800 feet).

&

For six months, the free-floating eggs and larvae
can travel up to several hundred miles, cradled by the
currents. During their early development, halibut
transform from a round fish into a flatfish.
The skull twists and one eye migrates to
a point adjacent to the other eye.

&

Young halibut rise to the surface and are
carried to shallower waters by prevailing currents.
Beginning their life as bottom dwellers, most
young halibut spend from five to seven years
in shallow nursery grounds.

&

No deep-fryer, no problem. Use this recipe the next time you have a craving for fish and chips. Serve with lemon slices, tartar sauce, and a creamy coleslaw. Serves 4

OVEN-BAKED HALIBUT & CHIPS

INGREDIENTS

3	medium baking potatoes	3
3 Tbsp	vegetable oil	45 mL
to taste	salt	to taste
4	5- to 6-oz (150- to 175-g) halibut fillets	4

METHOD

Preheat the oven to 425°F (220°C). Cut the potatoes in half lengthwise. Cut each half into 4 to 6 wedges and toss with the oil and seasoned salt. Arrange the potatoes in a single layer on a large non-stick or parchment-lined baking sheet. Bake for 15 minutes. Turn the potatoes over and bake for 5 minutes more. Sprinkle the fish with seasoned salt. Make a spot for each piece of fish among the potatoes. Continue baking until the fish is cooked through, about 10 to 15 minutes more.

A little bit cheeky and a whole lot good. I've considered using sour cream and onion flavored chips but haven't got around to it. One of the best things about this (besides eating it) is squishing the bag of potato chips to turn them into crumbs. This is one of the most requested recipes at the Fish House in Stanley Park, Vancouver.
Serves 6

HALIBUT & "CHIPS"

INGREDIENTS

½ cup	prepared mayonnaise	125 mL
1 Tbsp	Dijon mustard	15 mL
¼ tsp	garlic powder	1 mL
1¼ tsp	lemon juice	6 mL
1	3½-oz (100-g) bag plain potato chips	1
1 cup	panko (Japanese breadcrumbs)	250 mL
6	6-oz (175-g) halibut fillets	6

METHOD

Preheat the oven to 350°F (180°C). Combine the mayonnaise, mustard, garlic powder, and lemon juice in a shallow bowl. Mix well.

Coarsely crush the potato chips by squashing them in the bag. Add the panko and shake well. Spread out onto a plate. Dip the halibut fillets into the mayonnaise mixture, coating them on all sides. Dip all the sides into the potato chip mixture, patting gently to help the coating adhere. Place in a single layer on a baking sheet and bake for 15 to 20 minutes, until the halibut is cooked through and the crust is golden brown. Serve with lemon wedges, cocktail sauce, or malt vinegar.

The halibut may be cooked on the grill if you prefer. Try frying the capers until crisp for a different flavor and texture. Serves 4

BAKED HALIBUT

WITH LEMON BASIL VINAIGRETTE

INGREDIENTS

4	6-oz (175-g) fresh halibut fillets	4
to taste	sea salt and freshly ground black pepper	to taste
2 Tbsp	freshly squeezed lemon juice	30 mL
¼ tsp	sea salt	1 mL
1 tsp	grated lemon zest	5 mL
2	cloves garlic, cut in half	2
2 Tbsp	extra virgin olive oil	30 mL
3 Tbsp	fresh basil leaves, thinly sliced	45 mL
1 Tbsp	drained capers	15 mL

METHOD

Preheat the oven to 350°F (180°C). Season the halibut fillets with salt and pepper to taste. Lightly oil a baking dish and lay the halibut in the dish, without overlapping. Bake until the fish is cooked through, about 10 to 15 minutes.

While the fish is baking, make the vinaigrette. Combine the lemon juice, salt, pepper, and lemon zest in a small bowl. Spear the garlic on the tines of a fork and use it to beat the lemon juice mixture. Beat in the olive oil, basil, and capers. Place the halibut on heated plates, spoon the vinaigrette over it, and serve.

This halibut and lemony sauce make "fish night" very special. The chips, made from a variety of root vegetables, is texturally and visually pleasing. Serves 4

NEW AGE FISH & CHIPS
WITH A CHUNKY CITRUS TARTAR SAUCE

INGREDIENTS

Chunky Citrus Tartar Sauce

1 cup	sour cream	250 mL
1 cup	mayonnaise	250 mL
2 Tbsp	green relish	30 mL
2	lemons, juice of	2
3 Tbsp	finely chopped fresh parsley	45 mL
3 Tbsp	finely chopped fresh chives	45 mL
¼ cup	small capers, drained	60 mL
¼ cup	finely diced black olives	60 mL
2	small tomatoes, finely diced	2
2 Tbsp	chopped fresh tarragon	30 mL
1	small onion, finely diced	1
¼ cup	chopped fresh dill	60 mL
to taste	salt and black pepper	to taste

continues on next page

METHOD

Chunky Citrus Tartar Sauce

In a bowl, whisk together the sour cream, mayonnaise, green relish, and lemon juice. Fold in the remaining vegetables and herbs. Taste and season. This should be made at least an hour or two ahead to give time for the flavors to marry.

Root Vegetable Chips

Use as many or as few of these kinds of root vegetables as you like. Peel and then slice them paper thin—try a mandolin! Heat the oil to 310°F (155°C) and slowly deep-fry the vegetables, a few at a time, for about 1 minute, until golden brown and crispy. Remove to a paper towel to absorb any excess oil and, while still hot, season with salt and pepper. Be careful: the high sugar content in the carrots, parsnips, and sweet potatoes makes them easy to burn. Place in a warm oven or store them in an airtight container and reheat in

Root Vegetable Chips

1	Yukon Gold potato	1
1	russet potato	1
1	parsnip	1
1	carrot	1
1	sweet potato	1
1	plantain, still green	1
1	lotus root	1
	oil for deep-frying	
to taste	salt and white pepper	to taste

Halibut

4	6-oz (175-g) halibut fillets, skinless	4
to taste	salt and pepper	to taste
1 Tbsp	paprika	15 mL
1 cup	flour	250 mL
1 cup	olive oil	250 mL
2 Tbsp	unsalted butter	30 mL

a 350°F (180°C) oven for 5 minutes.

Halibut

Preheat the oven to 400°F (200°C). Season the halibut with the salt, pepper, and paprika to suit your taste, then dredge in flour. Pat off any excess flour. In a large ovenproof frying pan, heat the olive oil and sear the halibut about 2 minutes on one side. Add the butter and turn the fish over and cook the other side for about 2 minutes for a great texture and a crispy crust. Bake in the oven for 5 minutes, or until it reaches an internal temperature of 140°F (60°C). Remove from the pan and pat off any excess oil.

To serve, mound a handful of chips onto each plate. Place the fish on the chips and top with a large dollop of tartar sauce.

I like to serve halibut with a tasty sauce or salsa to bring out its flavors. I love to use Vidalia, Walla Walla, Maui, or Bermuda onions in this recipe. If you don't want to use jalapeño peppers, substitute ½ tsp (2 mL) hot chili sauce. *Serves 4*

HALIBUT

WITH TOMATO-LIME SALSA

INGREDIENTS

4	1½-lb (750-g) halibut steaks	4

Tomato-Lime Salsa

1	large ripe field tomato, seeded and chopped	1
½ cup	diced sweet onion	125 mL
2 Tbsp	freshly squeezed lime or lemon juice	30 mL
1 Tbsp	low-sodium soy sauce	15 mL
2 tsp	olive oil	10 mL
1 tsp	finely diced jalapeño pepper, seeded	5 mL
1 tsp	crushed garlic	5 mL
1 tsp	crushed fresh ginger	5 mL
pinch	salt	pinch
pinch	freshly ground black pepper	pinch
3 Tbsp	chopped cilantro or parsley	45 mL

METHOD

Preheat the oven to 425°F (220°C). Spray a baking sheet with vegetable spray.

To make the salsa, combine the tomato, onion, lime juice, soy sauce, olive oil, jalapeño pepper, garlic, ginger, salt, pepper, and cilantro. Either grill or bake the halibut for 10 to 15 minutes. Serve with the salsa overtop.

Prepare this dish and enjoy restaurant-style elegance in less than 30 minutes. Serves 8

ROASTED HALIBUT
WITH SAFFRON-CITRUS GLAZE

INGREDIENTS

Saffron-Citrus Glaze

1½ cups	fish or light chicken broth	375 mL
1 cup	orange juice	250 mL
½ cup	vermouth or sherry	125 mL
2 tsp	grated orange peel	10 mL
½ tsp	saffron threads	2 mL
2 Tbsp	cold butter, cubed	30 mL
to taste	salt and pepper	to taste

Fish

2 Tbsp	fresh bread crumbs	30 mL
2 Tbsp	almonds	30 mL
1 tsp	grated orange peel	5 mL
1 tsp	chopped fresh thyme	5 mL
¼ tsp	each salt and pepper	1 mL
2 Tbsp	melted butter	30 mL
8	6-oz (175-g) halibut fillets, 1 inch (2.5 cm) thick	8

METHOD

Combine the broth, orange juice, vermouth, orange peel, and saffron in a wide saucepan. Bring to a boil and cook for about 15 minutes or until reduced to about 1 cup (250 mL). Reduce the heat to low and slowly whisk in the butter, cube by cube. Season with salt and pepper. Keep the sauce warm. Preheat the oven to 450°F (230°C).

Combine the bread crumbs, almonds, orange peel, thyme, and salt and pepper in a food processor. Process until the almonds are the size of crumbs.

Brush one side of each fillet with butter. Press the buttered side of the fish into the crumb mixture to coat evenly. Transfer to a lightly greased baking sheet and cook for 12 to 15 minutes or until the flesh flakes easily with a fork and the topping is evenly browned.

Transfer the cooked fish to serving plates and spoon an equal amount of glaze around each piece.

The sweetness of corn matches well with the delicate flavor of halibut. Using a Chardonnay without a lot of oak for the sauce will bring out the character of this dish. If fresh corn isn't available, use good-quality frozen corn and add about 2 Tbsp (30 mL) water or stock to the sauce in place of the sugary liquid that's produced when corn kernels are removed. Serves 6

ROASTED HALIBUT
WITH CORN CHARDONNAY BUTTER

INGREDIENTS

6	6-oz (175-g) fresh halibut fillets	6
2 Tbsp	olive oil, for brushing	30 mL
1½ tsp	finely chopped fresh thyme, divided	7 mL
1	lemon, juice of	1
1 cup	Chardonnay	250 mL
1	shallot, minced	1
1 cup	fresh corn, removed from the cob, liquid reserved	250 mL
½ cup	unsalted butter, cut into pieces and chilled	125 mL
to taste	salt and pepper	to taste

METHOD

Preheat the oven to 375°F (190°C). Lightly oil a baking sheet or line with parchment paper. Place the halibut on the pan and lightly brush the fish with oil, then sprinkle it with salt, pepper, and ½ of the thyme. Roast for 10 to 15 minutes, until the fish layers just pull away when touched with a fork. Sprinkle the fish with lemon juice immediately before serving.

Meanwhile, prepare the sauce by placing the Chardonnay, shallot, and reserved juice from the corn cobs into a small pan. Simmer until the liquid is reduced by half. Add the corn and remaining thyme and bring to a simmer again. Reduce the heat to low and add the cold butter 1 piece at a time, stirring until all the butter is incorporated. Season with salt and pepper and serve over the halibut.

This recipe was inspired by a dish from New York's Jean-Georges Vongerichten. I made it for a class on how to make fish fabulous—and it really does. The nut crust adds new dimensions and bumps up the fish several levels, from straightforward to extraordinary. Serves 4

HALIBUT

WITH MUSTARD NUT CRUST

INGREDIENTS

4 Tbsp	butter, softened, divided	60 mL
¼ cup	whole grain mustard	60 mL
½ cup	hazelnuts, skinned and roughly ground	125 mL
4	6-oz (175-g) halibut fillets, 1 inch (2.5 cm) thick	4
to taste	kosher salt	to taste
to taste	cayenne pepper	to taste
3 Tbsp	chopped fresh thyme	45 mL
1½ cups	white wine	375 mL
½ cup	black olives, preferably niçoise	125 mL
4–5	sprigs thyme	4–5

METHOD

Preheat the oven to 500°F (260°C). Prepare the crust mixture by combining 3 Tbsp (45 mL) of the softened butter with the mustard and hazelnuts. Season the halibut with salt and cayenne pepper. Spread the crust mixture evenly over the top of each piece of halibut.

Heat an ovenproof pan (large enough to hold the fish without crowding) and add the remaining 1 Tbsp (15 mL) butter. Place the fish in the pan. Sprinkle with the chopped thyme and pour enough wine around the fish to come half way up the fillets and not touch the crust. Spread the olives and the thyme sprigs around the fish.

Bring the pan to a boil on top of the stove, then place it in the oven for about 10 to 15 minutes. Change the oven setting to broil and cook for another 2 minutes or until the crust is bubbly. Serve immediately.

Lavender is widely used in Provence to flavor foods—everything from fish to tapenade. Use it carefully or your food will taste like granny's soap. Perhaps each mouthful of food should have but one tiny speck of lavender on it. Adding lavender is optional but fun to try. In any case, the combination of fish, fennel, and orange works like a dream. Serves 4

HALIBUT

WITH BRAISED FENNEL & BLOOD ORANGE SAUCE

INGREDIENTS

4	5-oz (150-g) fresh halibut fillets	4
¾ tsp	sea salt	4 mL
pinch	freshly ground black pepper	pinch
1 Tbsp	extra virgin olive oil	15 mL
pinch	lavender (optional)	pinch
½ tsp	very finely chopped blood orange zest	2 mL
1	fennel bulb	1
1 Tbsp	unsalted butter	15 mL
2 Tbsp	water	30 mL
2 Tbsp	sliced fresh basil	30 mL
½ cup	blood orange juice	125 mL
2 tsp	raspberry or red wine vinegar	10 mL
2 Tbsp	unsalted butter	30 mL
4	whole leaves fresh basil	4

METHOD

Sprinkle the halibut with salt. Dust with a tiny pinch of pepper. Drizzle with the olive oil and sprinkle with lavender, if desired, and blood orange zest. Let sit for 1 hour.

Preheat the oven to 350°F (180°C). Trim the tops off the fennel. Trim the base and cut in half. Remove and discard the core and dice the bulb into ½-inch (1-cm) pieces. Warm a small saucepan over medium heat, add the 1 Tbsp (15 mL) of butter and the fennel. Cook and stir for 2 minutes. Add the water and a bit of salt and pepper. Cover and turn the heat down to low. Cook for 10 minutes or until tender. If it gets dry, add a splash of water. Stir in the sliced basil and keep warm.

Combine the blood orange juice and vinegar in a small saucepan. Place over medium heat and boil gently until reduced by half. Whisk in the 2 Tbsp (30 mL) of butter and a little salt and pepper. Keep warm.

Roast the halibut in the preheated oven for 10 to 15 minutes, or until cooked through. It should be barely firm in the centre and flaking at the edges.

To serve, arrange a mound of fennel in the centre of a warm plate, top with a piece of halibut, and drizzle the sauce around the outside. Garnish with a leaf of basil.

If you have some caponata in the freezer, you can dine on this chic black and white fish dish, with Mediterranean cachet, in less than 30 minutes. This dish is just right with a crisp Sauvignon Blanc or unoaked Chardonnay. Nice with roasted potatoes or some creamy polenta. Serves 2

BAKED HALIBUT
WITH TAPENADE CRUST & CAPONATA

INGREDIENTS

¾ lb	halibut fillet	375 g
⅓ cup	pitted kalamata olives	75 mL
1 Tbsp	extra virgin olive oil	15 mL
1 cup	Caponata	250 mL

Caponata
Makes 6 cups (1.5 L)

2 lb	eggplant, skin on, cubed	1 kg
1 lb	zucchini or other summer squash, cubed	500 g
2 tsp	salt	10 mL
½ cup	extra virgin olive oil	125 mL
1	large onion, chopped (about 2 cups/500 mL)	1
4	large cloves garlic, minced	4
1	red bell pepper, chopped	1
1	yellow bell pepper, chopped	1
1	14-oz (398-mL) can Roma tomatoes, chopped or puréed	1

METHOD

Preheat the oven to 325°F (160°C). Trim the edges of the fillet to create an even piece, about 1 inch (2.5 cm) thick. Cut the fillet into two equal squares. Set the fish aside on a baking sheet lined with parchment paper.

In a blender, purée the olives with the olive oil to form a very smooth paste. Press through a fine sieve if necessary to remove any bigger bits. Using a spatula or flexible knife, frost the top of each piece of fish with the olive paste, keeping it even and clean on the edges.

Bake the fish for 10 to 15 minutes, until just barely cooked through. Meanwhile, heat the caponata. To serve, place some caponata in the center of each plate and balance a piece of fish on top.

Caponata

Put the eggplant and zucchini cubes in a colander. Toss with the salt and set in the sink to drain for half an hour. Rinse quickly and pat dry.

continues on next page

Caponata is an addictive chunky condiment with roots in spicy Sicily that is great to serve antipasto style. Serve with a loaf of crusty bread, like ciabatta, for a hearty snack, or toss it with hot pasta and shredded Parmesan cheese for an exquisite vegetarian entrée. It's also wonderful spooned over a piece of grilled halibut or stirred into rice. Make caponata when eggplants, peppers, and squash are available at the market in August. Put it in jars or containers and freeze it for instant eating any time. Equally delicious hot or at room temperature.

INGREDIENTS — continued

1 Tbsp	brown sugar	15 mL
¼ cup	tomato paste	60 mL
3 Tbsp	balsamic vinegar	45 mL
½ cup	black olives, pitted and chopped	125 mL
2–3 Tbsp	chopped fresh basil or rosemary	30–45 mL
to taste	salt and freshly ground black pepper	to taste
	hot sauce (optional)	

METHOD — continued

Heat the oil in a large sauté pan or Dutch oven over medium heat. Add the onion, garlic, and peppers and sauté for 5 minutes. Add the eggplant and zucchini cubes and sauté for 5 to 10 minutes longer, until the mixture begins to soften. Stir in the tomatoes, cover the pan, and cook together for 10 minutes. Remove the lid and continue to simmer until the vegetables are very soft and the liquid in the pan has been reduced, about 5 minutes longer.

Whisk together the brown sugar, tomato paste, and vinegar. Add to the pan and mix well. Stir in the olives. Remove from the heat and add the fresh herbs. Season with salt and pepper (and a little hot sauce if you like it spicy). Cool to room temperature and serve. Refrigerated caponata will keep for a week, or it can be frozen.

The salty tang of pancetta and the smoked tomato vinaigrette are a wonderful match for the halibut.
Serves 6

PANCETTA-WRAPPED HALIBUT
WITH SMOKED TOMATO VINAIGRETTE

INGREDIENTS

6	5- to 6-oz (150- to 175-g) halibut fillets	6
to taste	sea salt and freshly ground black pepper	to taste
12	thin slices pancetta	12
1 Tbsp	vegetable oil	15 mL

Smoked Tomato Vinaigrette

6	canned plum tomatoes, well drained	6
2 tsp	cider vinegar	10 mL
pinch	freshly ground black pepper	pinch
¼ tsp	liquid smoke	1 mL
1	medium clove garlic, minced	1
½ tsp	sea salt	2 mL
½ cup	extra virgin olive oil	125 mL

METHOD

Lightly salt and pepper both sides of the halibut. Place 2 pieces of pancetta on one side of the halibut, slightly overlapping.

Preheat the oven to 350°F (180°C). Heat the vegetable oil in a large frying pan over medium heat. Slip in the halibut, pancetta side down. Fry until the pancetta is lightly browned. Flip the halibut over and fry until the bottom is lightly browned.

Transfer to a baking sheet, pancetta side up, and bake until the halibut just turns opaque, 10 to 15 minutes, depending on the thickness.

Serve on warm plates or a platter, drizzled with or surrounded by the vinaigrette.

Smoked Tomato Vinaigrette

Combine the tomatoes, vinegar, pepper, and liquid smoke in a food processor or blender. Mash the garlic to a paste with some of the salt. Add the garlic along with the remaining salt to the ingredients and blend until puréed. With the motor on, add the olive oil in a slow steady stream. Store covered and refrigerated for up to 3 weeks.

KAREN'S NOTE

This is an absolutely great vinaigrette. In a restaurant kitchen, it's easy to smoke the tomatoes over alder chips, but it's a messy and smoky process at home. I've cheated here and used canned tomatoes and liquid smoke—with no apologies.

Halibut is perfect with the traditional sauce and garnish for osso bucco. Serve with a saffron risotto.
Serves 6

HALIBUT "OSSO BUCCO"

INGREDIENTS

4 Tbsp	unsalted butter	60 mL
1 cup	finely chopped onion	250 mL
2/3 cup	finely chopped carrots	150 mL
2/3 cup	finely chopped celery	150 mL
1 Tbsp	finely chopped parsley	15 mL
2	medium cloves garlic, minced	2
2	strips lemon peel, peeled from a lemon with a vegetable peeler	2
2	bay leaves	2
1½ cups	canned tomatoes, with juice, puréed and sieved to remove the seeds	375 mL
1 cup	white wine	250 mL
3 cups	beef or chicken stock	750 mL
to taste	sea salt and freshly ground black pepper	to taste
2 Tbsp	finely chopped parsley	30 mL
2 tsp	lemon peel, grated	10 mL

continues on next page

METHOD

To make the sauce, melt the butter over medium heat in a large saucepan. Add the onion, carrot, celery, and parsley and sauté until the vegetables are soft but not browned, 8 to 10 minutes.

Add the 2 cloves of garlic, lemon peel strips, bay leaves, tomatoes, wine, and stock. Bring to a boil, then reduce to a simmer. Cook for about 1½ hours, stirring occasionally until reduced by two-thirds and thickened. Season with salt and pepper and remove from the heat. (The sauce may be prepared up to 2 days in advance. When cool, cover and refrigerate.)

When you're ready to finish the dish, combine the parsley, grated lemon peel, and ½ tsp (2 mL) of garlic in a small bowl and set aside.

Preheat the oven to 350°F (180°C). Salt and pepper the halibut. Heat the vegetable oil in a large, heavy frying pan over medium heat. Dip the halibut into the flour and shake off the excess.

½ tsp	garlic, minced	2 mL
6	6-oz (175-g) halibut fillets	6
to taste	salt and pepper	to taste
2 Tbsp	vegetable oil	30 mL
½ cup	all-purpose flour	125 mL

Fry until golden brown on both sides, turning once.

Remove from the pan and place in a single layer in a baking dish. Heat the sauce to a boil and pour over the halibut. Bake for 10 to 15 minutes. Sprinkle the parsley, garlic, and lemon garnish over the halibut and serve immediately.

Very simple, very tasty. Serves 4

HALIBUT
WITH PINE NUT & PARMESAN CRUST

INGREDIENTS

½ cup	pine nuts, coarsely chopped	125 mL
½ cup	freshly grated Parmesan cheese	125 mL
2 Tbsp	fresh basil, finely chopped	30 mL
1	clove garlic, minced	1
2 Tbsp	extra virgin olive oil	30 mL
4	6-oz (175-g) halibut fillets	4
to taste	sea salt	to taste

METHOD

Preheat the oven to 425°F (220°C). Combine the pine nuts, Parmesan cheese, basil, garlic, and olive oil. Place the halibut fillets on a baking sheet and season with salt. Pat the pine nut mixture onto the halibut, pressing lightly to make it stick. Bake in the middle of the oven for 10 to 15 minutes, until the fish is opaque all the way through.

A recipe guaranteed to wow your friends! Serves 8

BAKED HALIBUT
WITH PISTACHIO CRUST & ORANGE BASIL SAUCE

INGREDIENTS

2 cups	pistachios, coarsely ground	500 mL
2 cups	panko (Japanese breadcrumbs)	500 mL
6	egg whites, lightly beaten	6
8	4-oz (100-g) halibut fillets	8
to taste	salt and freshly ground white pepper	to taste
4 Tbsp	vegetable oil	60 mL

Orange Basil Sauce

2 cups	orange juice	500 mL
1 cup	white wine	250 mL
2 Tbsp	honey	30 mL
1 cup	whipping cream	250 mL
2 tsp	chopped orange rind	10 mL
½ cup	orange segments	125 mL
to taste	salt and black pepper	to taste

METHOD

Preheat the oven to 350°F (180°C). Mix together the pistachios and panko on a plate. Put the egg whites in a shallow pan. Season the fillets to taste with salt and white pepper. Dip 1 side of each fillet in the egg white, then into the pistachio-breadcrumb mixture to make a crust. Heat the oil in a sauté pan and sear the crusted sides of the fillets. Place them on a baking sheet and finish in the oven for 15 to 18 minutes or until the fish is flaky.

Serve on a platter and drizzle the Orange Basil Sauce over and around the fish.

Orange Basil Sauce

In a saucepan, combine the orange juice, white wine, honey, and whipping cream. Bring to a boil, then reduce the heat and add the orange rind and segments. Season to taste with salt and pepper. Continue to cook until the sauce reduces by about one third.

Serve this with basmati rice and a cucumber salad. Serves 6

HALIBUT

WITH COCONUT CILANTRO CHUTNEY

INGREDIENTS

1 cup	shredded dried unsweetened coconut	250 mL
½ cup	cilantro leaves, packed	125 mL
4 Tbsp	water	60 mL
1	hot chili, chopped	1
1	½-inch (1-cm) piece ginger, peeled and smashed	1
1	clove garlic, chopped	1
6 Tbsp	yogurt	90 mL
1 Tbsp	lemon juice	15 mL
to taste	sea salt	to taste
6	6-oz (175-g) halibut fillets, about 1 inch (2.5 cm) thick	6

METHOD

Preheat the oven to 400°F (200°C). In a food processor, blend the coconut, cilantro, water, chili, ginger, and garlic to a paste. Add the yogurt, lemon juice, and salt. Pulse to combine and transfer to a bowl.

Lay the halibut on a baking pan and coat the top of the fillets with the chutney. Bake for 10 to 15 minutes, depending on the thickness, until the halibut is just opaque in the center.

I find that organic apple butter from natural food stores has the best flavor. You can use finely chopped sweet mango chutney instead of the apple butter. *Serves 4*

HALIBUT

WITH CURRIED APPLE BUTTER

INGREDIENTS

¼ cup	apple butter	60 mL
¼ cup	mayonnaise	60 mL
1 Tbsp	minced green onion	15 mL
½ tsp	good quality curry powder	2 mL
to taste	sea salt and freshly ground black pepper	to taste
4	6-oz (175-g) halibut fillets	4

METHOD

Preheat the oven to 400°F (200°C). In a small bowl, combine the apple butter, mayonnaise, onion, and curry powder. Season to taste and mix until well blended. Line a baking sheet with aluminum foil and place the fillets on top. Smooth the apple butter mixture on the tops of the halibut. Bake for 10 to 15 minutes until the fish just flakes when tested with a fork.

This dish is fast and dead easy, with loads of gourmet cachet. Stir up a pot of plain saffron risotto or sauté some spinach to serve alongside. Pure and so simple. Serves 4

ROASTED HALIBUT ITALIAN STYLE

INGREDIENTS

1 Tbsp	extra virgin olive oil	15 mL
1	clove garlic, crushed	1
¼ cup	pine nuts, ground	60 mL
¼ cup	finely grated Parmesan cheese	60 mL
1½ lb	boneless, skinless halibut fillet, cut into 4 portions	750 g
½ cup	basil pesto	125 mL
1	large tomato, thinly sliced	1
to taste	salt and freshly ground black pepper	to taste

METHOD

Preheat the oven to 450°F (230°C). In a small bowl, combine the olive oil, garlic, pine nuts, and Parmesan cheese. Arrange the fish on a shallow baking sheet lined with parchment paper. Smear each portion of fish with 1 Tbsp (15 mL) of pesto and top with a couple slices of tomato. Season with salt and pepper.

Press 2 Tbsp (30 mL) of the pine nut topping over each piece of fish. Place the baking sheet into the pre-heated oven and roast for 10 minutes, until the fish is just cooked through and the nuts are brown.

This is an interpretation of a dish I used to eat in a small Middle Eastern café in Toronto. Served with a tomato salad with mint, this is great for a buffet. Serves 6

BAKED HALIBUT
WITH LEMON, TAHINI & PINE NUTS

INGREDIENTS

2 lb	halibut fillets, cut into 2-inch (5-cm) chunks	1 kg
½ tsp	sea salt	2 mL
½ tsp	freshly ground black pepper	2 mL
pinch	cayenne	pinch
2 Tbsp	lemon juice	30 mL
3 Tbsp	extra virgin olive oil	45 mL
2	onions, thinly sliced into half-moons	2
2	cloves garlic, crushed to a paste with ½ tsp (2 mL) salt	2
½ cup	lemon juice	125 mL
½ cup	cold water	125 mL
½ cup	tahini	125 mL
2 Tbsp	pine nuts	30 mL
1 Tbsp	fresh parsley, coarsely chopped	15 mL

METHOD

Toss the fish with the salt, pepper, cayenne, and 2 Tbsp (30 mL) lemon juice. Cover and refrigerate for 1 hour.

In a large, non-stick frying pan, heat the olive oil over medium-low heat. Add the onion and cook until soft and a deep golden brown, about 15 minutes. Remove from the heat and set aside to drain on paper towels.

Place the tahini in a bowl. Slowly whisk in the garlic paste, ½ cup (125 mL) of lemon juice, and water until smooth and creamy. Set aside.

Preheat the oven to 375°F (190°C). Lightly oil a baking dish. Place the fish in the dish in a single layer, cover tightly with aluminum foil, and bake for 10 minutes. Remove the foil and bake for 5 to 10 minutes longer, until the fish is just cooked through. Drain off the juice that has accumulated around the fish and combine it with the tahini mixture.

Spread the tahini sauce over the fish and sprinkle with the onion, pine nuts, and parsley. Serve warm or at room temperature.

We all know about sour cream and chives on halved potatoes. Try it with halibut and serve a baked potato on the side. Serves 4

BAKED HALIBUT
WITH SOUR CREAM & CHIVES

INGREDIENTS

4	halibut fillets, about 1 inch (2.5 cm) thick	4
to taste	freshly ground black pepper	to taste
2 Tbsp	butter	30 mL
2 cups	sliced mushrooms	500 mL
1 cup	sour cream	250 mL
¼ cup	dry sherry	60 mL
4 Tbsp	chopped chives	60 mL

METHOD

Preheat the oven to 400°F (200°C). Put the halibut in a buttered 8- × 12-inch (20- × 30-cm) baking dish. Season with pepper. Melt the butter in a skillet over medium heat and sauté the mushrooms until softened. Add the sour cream, sherry, and chives to the skillet and mix together. Simmer for 1 minute, then pour the mixture over the halibut. Bake in the preheated oven for 10 to 15 minutes or until the fish flakes.

This is always an easy show-stopper, usually served to a chorus of "oohs" and "aahs." Don't forget to take a bow. Serves 4

HALIBUT BAKED IN CORN HUSKS
WITH CORN & ZUCCHINI SAUTÉ

INGREDIENTS

4	whole ears of corn	4
4	5- to 6-oz (150- to 175-g) halibut fillets	4
to taste	sea salt and freshly ground black pepper	to taste
4 Tbsp	unsalted butter	60 mL
1 cup	diced red onion	250 mL
1 cup	diced zucchini	250 mL

METHOD

Carefully peel back the corn husks and snap off the corn cob at the bottom, leaving the husks attached to the stem. Discard the silk and any blemished leaves. Set the husks aside. Cut 2 cups (500 mL) of kernels from the corn and set aside.

Preheat the oven to 350°F (180°C). Lightly salt and pepper the halibut. Tuck a fillet into the middle of each corn husk, enclosing it within the leaves. Don't try to make it look neat. Tear 4 strips from the discarded leaves and use them to tie the opened end of the husk. Place on a baking sheet and bake for 10 to 15 minutes.

While the halibut is baking, melt the butter in a saucepan over medium heat and sauté the red onions until they're translucent. Add the zucchini and sauté until it just begins to soften. Add the corn and continue to cook until it's heated through.

Place the halibut on heated plates. Fold back the top of the corn husks and tuck them under the stem. Spoon the corn sauté over the halibut. Serve immediately.

This recipe calls for cooking *en papillote*, which comes from the French word "papillon," which means butterfly. In this case, it's moisture-and-grease-resistant parchment paper, available pretty much anywhere. Serves 6

HALIBUT STEAKS
IN PARCHMENT WITH MUSHROOMS & TARRAGON

INGREDIENTS

6	6–8 oz (175–250 g) halibut fillets, 1 inch (2.5 cm) thick	6
	parchment paper	
6 Tbsp	melted butter	90 mL
3 cups	fresh sliced mushrooms	750 mL
6	fresh tarragon sprigs, tops reserved and leaves finely cut	6
1	lemon, juice of	1
to taste	salt and pepper	to taste
2	medium zucchini, sliced	2
3	egg whites, beaten	3

METHOD

Preheat the oven to 375°F (190°F). Rinse the halibut under cold water and pat dry with a paper towel. Set aside.

Fold a 15- × 13-inch (38- × 33-cm) piece of parchment paper in half crosswise to make a rectangle 13 × 7½ inches (33 × 19 cm). Draw a half heart, beginning and ending at the folded edge, and cut along the line. Repeat this so that you have 6 pieces of parchment ready to go. Open each paper and brush one half with some of the melted butter, leaving a 1-inch (2.5-cm) border unbuttered.

Combine the mushrooms, tarragon leaves, lemon juice, salt, and pepper in a bowl. Stir to coat the mushrooms. Spread the mushroom blend over the buttered portion of the parchment and set a halibut steak on top of each. Season the halibut with salt and pepper.

Arrange the zucchini slices on the fish by slightly overlapping them lengthways along the center of the fish. Top with the reserved tarragon tops.

Brush the edges of each piece of parchment paper with egg white and crimp the edges, ensuring they're all well sealed. Transfer the paper packages to a baking sheet. Bring the sheet to the heated oven and bake until the packages are puffed and light brown, about 10 to 15 minutes.

Transfer to dinner plates and serve. Pinch the top of the parchment and rip open just before serving for mouth-watering, aromatic steam.

Halibut cheeks are one of the real thrills of halibut season. I like them better than any other part of the fish. You can also use halibut fillets cut into 2 × 2 × 1-inch (5 × 5 × 2.5-cm) pieces for this dish. Serves 4

SCALLOPED HALIBUT CHEEKS

INGREDIENTS

1½ lb	large halibut cheeks	750 g
to taste	sea salt and freshly ground black pepper	to taste
½ cup	flour	125 mL
1 cup	whipping cream	250 mL
1 Tbsp	fresh dill	15 mL
1	green onion, minced	1
2 Tbsp	lemon juice	30 mL
¼ tsp	sea salt	1 mL
1 Tbsp	butter, melted	15 mL
1¼ cups	soft white breadcrumbs	310 mL

TO MAKE SOFT WHITE BREADCRUMBS

Remove the crusts from a loaf of bread that's 1 or 2 days old and cut or tear it into 1-inch (2.5-cm) pieces. Place a handful into the bowl of a food processor and pulse until large soft crumbs form. I've done this even in a coffee grinder. It works well for small quantities of crumbs.

METHOD

Salt and pepper the halibut cheeks on both sides. Place the flour on a plate and dip the fish in the flour, coating both sides. Place the cheeks, keeping the smaller ones in the center, in a baking dish that will hold them snugly without overlapping.

Mix together the whipping cream, dill, onion, lemon juice, and ¼ tsp (1 mL) salt and pour over the halibut cheeks. Bake in the oven for 15 minutes.

While the cheeks are baking, mix together the melted butter and breadcrumbs. After 15 minutes, remove the dish from the oven and sprinkle the buttered breadcrumbs over the halibut cheeks. Try to get the crumbs mostly on the fish, not the cream. Return to the oven and bake for 15 minutes longer, or until the flesh is opaque. If the crumbs aren't quite browned, place the dish under the broiler until they turn a crunchy gold. Let the dish settle for a few minutes before serving.

PAN-ROASTED HALIBUT WITH LENTIL & TOMATO VINAIGRETTE | page 56

Karen Barnaby — *The Passionate Cook*

PUBLIC HOUSE FISH 'N' CHIPS | pages 74 – 75

PHOTO BY GEOFFREY ROSS • DIGITAL ARTIST JEFF MAYHEW • FOOD STYLING BY RYAN JENNINGS & DAVID STEELE

HALIBUT CHEEKS ROASTED ON POTATO CRISPS | page 113

Karen Barnaby — *Pacific Passions*

I think the cheeks are the most satisfying part of the fish. This recipe shows them off beautifully. Serves 4

HALIBUT CHEEKS
ROASTED ON POTATO CRISPS

INGREDIENTS

1½ lb	russet potatoes	750 g
⅓ cup	extra virgin olive oil, divided	75 mL
6	cloves garlic, cut in half	6
½ tsp	sea salt	2 mL
¼ tsp	pepper	1 mL
8	3- to 4-oz (75- to 100-g) halibut cheeks, or 5- to 6-oz (150- to 175-g) halibut fillets	8
to taste	sea salt and freshly ground black pepper	to taste
1	plum tomato, peeled, seeded, and diced	1
2	bay leaves, crumbled	2
4	sprigs fresh thyme	4
¼ tsp	fennel seeds	1 mL

METHOD

Preheat the oven to 425°F (220°C). Slice the potatoes very thinly, as if you were making potato chips. Wash the slices, drain them well, and dry with a towel. In a large bowl, combine the potatoes, 4 Tbsp (60 mL) of the olive oil, and the garlic, salt, and pepper. Toss well and spread evenly in a 9- × 13-inch (22- × 33-cm) baking pan (don't use a glass pan). Bake for 20 minutes, turning every 5 minutes.

Season the fish with salt, pepper, and the remaining 1 Tbsp (15 mL) of the olive oil. Scatter the tomato, bay leaves, thyme, and fennel seeds over the potatoes and place the fish on top. Bake for 5 minutes if using the cheeks, 10 minutes if using fillets.

Remove from the oven and preheat the broiler. Return to the oven and broil 8-inches (20-cm) from the heat until the potatoes around the edge of the dish turn crispy, about 5 minutes. Remove from the oven and serve immediately.

Baking fish in filo pastry keeps it moist. It also creates a crispy exterior that's hard to resist, particularly when paired with the rich and creamy sauce featured in this dish. Serves 2

HALIBUT & SPINACH WRAPPED IN FILO

INGREDIENTS

Fish

1	10-oz (300-g) package frozen chopped spinach, thawed	1
1 Tbsp	butter	15 mL
1	shallot, finely chopped	1
1	clove garlic, crushed	1
4	sheets filo pastry	4
2–3 Tbsp	melted butter	30–45 mL
2	6-oz (175-g) halibut fillets	2
to taste	salt and freshly ground black pepper	to taste

continues on next page

METHOD

Fish

Squeeze as much moisture from the spinach as you can and set aside. Heat the 1 Tbsp (15 mL) butter in a small skillet over medium heat. Add the shallot and garlic and cook until softened, about 1 to 2 minutes. Add the spinach and season with salt and pepper. Remove from the heat and set aside. Preheat the oven to 400°F (200°C).

Lay a sheet of filo pastry on your work surface. Brush lightly with melted butter. Top with another sheet and brush again. Repeat the process until all the sheets are used. Cut the stacked sheets in half. Divide the spinach mixture and place near the bottom centre of each sheet. Set the halibut on top of the spinach and season with salt and pepper. Fold the sides of the filo over to partially cover the halibut and then roll it up to form a package and seal the filling inside. Place on

Sauce

1 Tbsp	butter	15 mL
1	shallot, finely chopped	1
2 Tbsp	lemon juice	30 mL
¾ cup	whipping cream	175 mL
2 Tbsp	capers	30 mL
1 Tbsp	chopped chives	15 mL
to taste	salt and freshly ground black pepper	to taste

a parchment-lined baking tray. Brush the tops with butter. Place on the middle rack in the oven for 20 to 25 minutes.

Sauce

While the fish cooks, make the sauce. Melt the butter in a pot set over medium heat. Add the shallot and cook until softened, about 1 to 2 minutes. Add the lemon juice and continue cooking until it has almost all evaporated. Pour in the cream and cook until it thickens slightly. Add the capers and chives. Season with salt and pepper.

To serve, pour a pool of the sauce on 2 dinner plates. Cut each filo parcel in half at a slight angle. Arrange the pieces over the sauce.

Impress your friends with this gorgeous main course. It's much easier to make than the finished product suggests. Serves 8

HALIBUT PARCELS
WITH TOMATO CILANTRO SAUCE

INGREDIENTS

⅔ cup	halved and seeded tomatoes (about 3 Roma tomatoes)	150 mL
6 Tbsp	chopped cilantro	90 mL
2 Tbsp	garlic, crushed	30 mL
1 Tbsp	ginger, grated	15 mL
4 Tbsp	green onions, chopped	60 mL
1 Tbsp	sesame oil	15 mL
8	4-oz (100-g) halibut fillets	8
8	sheets rice paper in 10-inch (25-cm) rounds	8
2 Tbsp	vegetable oil	30 mL
1 cup	white wine	250 mL
½ cup	fish stock (see page 176)	125 mL
6 Tbsp	butter, cubed	90 mL

METHOD

Preheat the oven to 350°C (180°F). Place the tomatoes on a baking sheet and bake until they're dry, 30 to 40 minutes. Cool and coarsely chop. In a food processor or blender, mix the cilantro, garlic, ginger, and green onion. Blend in the sesame oil until a paste forms. (Set aside 2 Tbsp/30 mL of this paste for the sauce.) Spread the paste evenly over one side of each fish fillet.

Working with one sheet of rice paper at a time, soak it for 15 to 20 seconds in warm water. Place it on a clean surface and top it with a piece of halibut in the center. Fold the bottom, sides, and top over to completely wrap the halibut.

In a very hot sauté pan, heat the oil and sear the parcels. Finish them in the oven for about 10 minutes, or until they're lightly browned.

In a sauté pan, sauté the 2 Tbsp (30 mL) of reserved paste with the roasted tomatoes. Add the white wine and fish stock and bring to a boil. Reduce the heat and swirl in the butter. To serve, place the parcels on a platter and pour the sauce over and around them.

Easy and delicious. Serves 4

CHILI LIME HALIBUT TACOS

INGREDIENTS

4	4-oz (100-g) halibut fillets	4
1 Tbsp	olive oil	15 mL
1	lime, juice of	1
½ tsp	ground cumin	2 mL
½ tsp	chili powder	2 mL
½ tsp	oregano	2 mL
pinch	cayenne pepper	pinch
to taste	salt and pepper	to taste
8	taco shells	8
2 cups	shredded lettuce	500 mL
1	medium avocado, sliced into wedges	1
1 cup	salsa	250 mL

METHOD

Preheat the oven to 425°F (220°C). Place the halibut in a non-stick or parchment-lined baking dish. Drizzle with the olive oil and lime juice; sprinkle with the spices and herbs. Bake for 12 to 15 minutes, or until just cooked through. Remove from the oven and cool slightly. While cooling, heat the taco shells in the oven for a few minutes. Coarsely flake the fish. Stuff the taco shells with lettuce, avocado, salsa, and flaked fish. Serve.

This lasagna is rich and decadent enough to serve on any special occasion. Serve it with a mixed green or caesar salad. Serves 8

SENSATIONAL SEAFOOD LASAGNA

INGREDIENTS

2½ cups	fish stock (see page 176), or chicken stock	625 mL
1½ cups	light cream or milk	375 mL
2	cloves garlic, finely chopped	2
⅓ cup	all-purpose flour	75 mL
to taste	salt and white pepper	to taste
pinch	ground nutmeg	pinch
½ lb	firm halibut fillets, cut into small cubes	250 g
1	1-lb (500-g) tub ricotta cheese	1
2	large eggs	2
½ cup	chopped fresh basil	125 mL
½ lb	cooked salad shrimp	250 g
1 cup	fresh or canned crabmeat	250 mL
¾–1 lb	mozzarella cheese, shredded	375–500 g
½ cup	freshly grated Parmesan cheese	125 mL
1	1-lb (500-g) box lasagna noodles, cooked	1
for garnish	basil sprigs	for garnish

METHOD

Place 2 cups (500 mL) of the stock in a pot. Add the cream and garlic, and bring to a simmer. Mix the remaining stock with the flour until smooth. Slowly whisk into the stock mixture. Bring back to a simmer and cook until the sauce thickens. Season with the salt, pepper, and nutmeg; mix in the cubed fish. Remove from the heat and set aside. (The fish will cook through when baked in the lasagna.)

Combine the ricotta cheese with the eggs and basil. Season with salt and pepper and set aside. Preheat the oven to 350°F (180°C).

To assemble the lasagna, spoon a little sauce into the bottom of a 9- × 13-inch (3.5-L) casserole dish. Top with 4 noodles, ⅓ of the remaining sauce, and ½ of the shrimp and crab (squeezed dry). Sprinkle with ⅓ of the mozzarella and Parmesan cheeses. Top with another layer of noodles and then with the ricotta cheese mixture. Top with another layer of noodles, another ⅓ of the sauce, the rest of the shrimp and crab, and another ⅓ of the cheeses. Top with 4 more noodles and the remaining sauce and cheese. Bake—tented with foil so it doesn't touch the cheese—for 40 minutes. Uncover and bake for another 15 to 20 minutes, until brown and bubbly. Let the lasagna rest for 5 to 10 minutes before slicing and serving.

ERIC'S TIP

This lasagna can be made oven-ready several hours in advance. Cool to room temperature after assembling, then wrap and refrigerate until ready to bake. Add 10 more minutes baking time, as you'll be starting it from cold. For even richer-tasting lasagna, replace the mozzarella cheese with a more complex-tasting Italian-style cheese, such as provolone or Asiago.

Be careful not to overcook the halibut. I find that one minute too long can make the difference between moist or dry fish. It's best to use fresh halibut for perfect results. Serves 6–8

HALIBUT

WITH LEMON GINGER CHILI MARINADE

INGREDIENTS

1 Tbsp	finely minced lemon peel	15 mL
⅓ cup	freshly squeezed lemon juice	75 mL
½ cup	dry white wine	125 mL
2 Tbsp	canola oil	30 mL
2 Tbsp	soy sauce	30 mL
1 Tbsp	oyster sauce	15 mL
½ tsp	Asian chili sauce	2 mL
1 Tbsp	finely minced fresh ginger, grated	15 mL
2	cloves garlic, crushed	2
2 lb	halibut fillets, cut into 6 pieces	1 kg

METHOD

To make the marinade, mix together all the ingredients, except the halibut, in a large bowl.

Marinate the fish for 15 to 20 minutes; turn to coat. Keep refrigerated until ready to cook. Broil 6 inches (15 cm) from the element, for 10 to 12 minutes, until the fish flakes. Continue to coat with the marinade as the fish cooks.

A quick and easy casserole that provides a tasty, healthy dinner for two, all in one pan. Serves 2

HALIBUT & FRESH VEGETABLE CASSEROLE

INGREDIENTS

8–12	small new potatoes, halved	8–12
1	medium carrot, thickly sliced	1
12–18	snow or snap peas, trimmed	12–18
2 Tbsp	olive oil or melted butter	30 mL
2	5- to 6-oz (150- to 175-g) halibut fillets	2
½	lemon, juice of	½
to taste	salt and freshly ground black pepper	to taste
1 Tbsp	chopped fresh parsley or other fresh herb	15 mL

METHOD

Preheat the oven to 425°F (220°C). Place the potatoes and carrots in a pot and cover with cold water. Bring to a boil and cook until firm-tender. Add the peas and cook just until they turn bright green. Drain the vegetables, immerse in cold water to cool, then drain again.

Brush a shallow baking dish with 1 Tbsp (15 mL) of the olive oil. Place the fish in the baking dish and surround with the cooked vegetables. Drizzle with the remaining oil or butter, sprinkle with lemon juice, and season with salt and pepper. Bake for 15 minutes, or until the fish is opaque and just begins to flake. Sprinkle with parsley and serve.

ERIC'S TIP

Try baking cooked and cooled green beans, asparagus spears, or cauliflower alongside the fish. To spice the dish up a bit, sprinkle the fish and vegetables before baking with Cajun spice or your favorite seafood spice blend.

Fish wrapped in prosciutto is done in so many restaurants—although its origins are uncertain—it makes for an impressive presentation and adds wonderful flavor. Serves 4

HALIBUT PROVENÇAL
WRAPPED IN PROSCIUTTO

INGREDIENTS

Vegetables

3 Tbsp	virgin olive oil	45 mL
1	onion, halved and slivered	1
1 lb	small new potatoes, cooked, cooled, and cut into thick slices	500 g
2	cloves garlic, minced	2
1	red or yellow bell pepper, slivered	1
1	14-oz (398-mL) can artichoke hearts, rinsed, drained, and quartered	1
½ cup	chicken broth	125 mL
1 Tbsp	lemon juice	15 mL
to taste	salt and freshly ground black pepper	to taste
¼ cup	air-cured black olives	60 mL

continues on next page

METHOD

In a sauté pan, heat the olive oil over medium heat and sauté the onion until it begins to brown. Add the potatoes and continue cooking until they're nicely browned. Add the garlic, bell pepper, and artichokes and continue to cook together, until the pepper is tender. Add the broth and lemon juice and simmer for 5 minutes, then stir in the salt and pepper. Arrange the vegetable mixture in a shallow oven-proof casserole dish (something pretty that you can bring to the table) and scatter black olives about.

Preheat the oven to 400°F (200°C). Season the fish lightly with salt, pepper, and cayenne pepper. If you've cut 5-oz (150-g) pieces from a thick halibut fillet, you should have rectangular fingers, each about 2 to 3 inches (5 to 8 cm) across. To wrap the fish pieces, lay two pieces of prosciutto on your work surface, overlapping slightly. Top with two large sage or basil leaves. Set a fish finger on top and wrap the prosciutto

Fish

4	5-oz (150-g) halibut fillets	4
to taste	salt, freshly ground black pepper, and cayenne pepper	to taste
8–10	paper-thin slices prosciutto	8–10
8	large fresh sage leaves, whole (or use whole basil leaves)	8
1 Tbsp	butter	15 mL
1 Tbsp	olive oil	15 mL
for garnish	fresh sage leaves (or basil), chopped	for garnish

tightly around it, enclosing the herbs and the fish inside. If the prosciutto is sliced thinly enough, it will wrap easily and stick to itself.

Heat the butter and oil together in a non-stick sauté pan over medium-high heat. When the pan is hot, add the fish and sauté for about 2 minutes on all sides, until the prosciutto is nicely browned and crisp and the fish is nearly cooked. Nestle the fish in the vegetables in the casserole dish. Place in the preheated oven and heat for 5 minutes longer, just until everything is heated through.

Strew a few chopped sage or basil leaves over top and serve your guests directly from the casserole dish at the table.

When a local fisherman shows up at my door with a fresh halibut, this is the gold standard recipe I usually cook up first. It's my favorite way to add simple, bright flavor to the firm, meaty fish. Serves 4

HALIBUT PROVENÇAL

INGREDIENTS

splash	extra virgin olive oil	splash
4	5- to 6-oz (150- to 175-g) fresh halibut fillets	4
to taste	salt and freshly ground black pepper	to taste
4	large ripe tomatoes, or one 28-oz (796-mL) can whole tomatoes	4
4	large cloves garlic, minced	4
1	large onion, minced	1
½ cup	capers	125 mL
½ cup	pitted calamata olives	125 mL
½ cup	pitted green olives	125 mL
1 Tbsp	balsamic vinegar	15 mL

METHOD

Preheat a large, heavy skillet over medium-high heat. Add a splash of olive oil (enough to cover the bottom of the pan with a light film). Pat the halibut fillets dry with a piece of paper towel and lightly season with salt and pepper. Place the fillets in the hot oil and brown on both sides.

Remove the fillets from the pan and add the remaining ingredients. Bring the mixture to a simmer and serve with the fish.

GRILLED

Up to 10 years of age, halibut are highly migratory,

generally traveling in a clockwise direction throughout

the Gulf of Alaska. Older halibut tend to settle down,

having a much smaller "home range" than younger fish.

༶

Halibut are a long-lived fish. Their growth rate varies,

depending on location and habitat conditions.

Females grow faster and live longer than males.

The oldest halibut on record was 55 years old.

༶

Halibut are the largest of all flatfish.

What might be the largest Pacific halibut

ever documented was pulled from the Bering Sea

off St. Paul Island on the 5th of September, 2003.

The eight-foot, two-inch halibut was

estimated at 533 pounds,

based on its length.

༶

The dense, meaty texture of halibut is best served by grilling, and it's enhanced by this simple seasonal salad. Use a mixture of blood oranges, grapefruit, oranges, tangerines, and tangelos. For an herbal note, use a high-quality oil infused with herbs. Serves 4

GRILLED HALIBUT
WITH TRIPLE CITRUS SALSA

INGREDIENTS

Salsa

4–5	mixed citrus fruits, peeled and segmented	4–5
2 Tbsp	fresh ginger, sliced into matchsticks	30 mL
1–2 Tbsp	herb-infused olive or avocado oil	15–30 mL
to taste	kosher salt and hot chili flakes	to taste
1–2 Tbsp	citrus juice	15–30 mL

Fish

4	5-oz (150-g) halibut steaks	4
1 Tbsp	grated fresh ginger	15 mL
½	lemon, zest only	½
to taste	hot chili flakes	to taste
2 Tbsp	olive oil	30 mL
1 Tbsp	minced fresh thyme or chives	15 mL

METHOD

Salsa

Combine all the ingredients for the salsa. Stir gently and store in the refrigerator until needed.

Fish

Preheat the grill to medium-high. Sprinkle the fish with the ginger, lemon zest, hot chili flakes, oil, and herbs. Place the fish on the grill and cook until just done, about 7 minutes per inch (2.5 cm), turning once. Serve with the salsa.

Many fruits don't work well with fish, but pineapple is a natural partner. Basmati rice and grilled zucchini complete the plate. Serves 4

GRILLED HALIBUT
WITH PINEAPPLE SALSA

INGREDIENTS		
½	pineapple, peeled, cored, and chopped	½
1	Granny Smith apple, cored and grated	1
1 tsp	grated fresh ginger	5 mL
½	lemon, juice and zest	½
to taste	salt and hot chili flakes	to taste
4	5-oz (150-g) halibut steaks	4
1 Tbsp	canola oil	15 mL
1 Tbsp	grated fresh ginger	15 mL
½	lemon, zest only	½
to taste	hot chili flakes	to taste
1 Tbsp	minced fresh thyme or chives	15 mL

METHOD

Combine the pineapple, apple, 1 tsp (5 mL) ginger, lemon juice and zest, salt, and hot chili flakes. Stir well, cover, and let stand to allow the flavors to blend.

Lightly oil the fish. Sprinkle it with the 1 Tbsp (15 mL) ginger, lemon zest, hot chili flakes, and thyme. Heat the grill to high and grill the fish, turning once. Serve with the pineapple compote on the side.

GRILLED HALIBUT WITH PINEAPPLE SALSA | page 128

dee Hobsbawn-Smith — *Quick Cuisine: Fabulous Meals in Minutes*

PHOTO BY KEN MCCURDY • FOOD STYLING BY DEE HOBSBAWN-SMITH

BAKED HALIBUT WITH TAPENADE CRUST & CAPONATA | page 96
Cinda Chavich — *The Girl Can't Cook*

HALIBUT BAKED IN CORN HUSKS WITH CORN & ZUCCHINI SAUTÉ | page 109

Karen Barnaby — *Pacific Passions*

SENSATIONAL SEAFOOD LASAGNA | pages 118–19

Eric Akis — *Everyone Can Cook Seafood*

Pink peppercorns are the dried berries of the Baies rose plant. This rose-hued spice isn't a true peppercorn and doesn't have the hot bite associated with that spice. They make a mildly spicy, slightly sweet and aromatic addition to this halibut dish. Serves 4

GRILLED HALIBUT STEAKS
WITH PINK PEPPERCORN CHIVE BUTTER

INGREDIENTS

¼ lb	butter, at room temperature	125 g
1 Tbsp	pink peppercorns, crushed	15 mL
2 Tbsp	chopped fresh chives	30 mL
1	small clove garlic, crushed	1
to taste	salt and freshly ground black pepper	to taste
4	5-oz (150-g) halibut fillets	4
2 Tbsp	olive oil	30 mL

METHOD

Beat the butter until light. Beat in the peppercorns, chives, garlic, salt, and pepper. Roll the flavored butter in parchment paper or foil to make a log about 1 inch (2.5 cm) thick in diameter. Refrigerate until set.

Preheat the grill to medium-high. Brush the halibut with oil and season with salt and pepper. Grill for 3 to 4 minutes per side, or until just cooked through. Top each fillet with 2 thick slices of the butter and serve.

ERIC'S TIP

Make mixed peppercorn butter by replacing half the pink peppercorns with lightly crushed green peppercorns. Replace the chives with 1 Tbsp (15 mL) chopped fresh tarragon for a pungent licorice-scented butter.

This unusual recipe, which I've adapted for the plank, pairs the intense flavor of the spiced halibut with a cool tropical salsa. Cuban-style black beans and rice go very well with this. Serves 4–6

PLANKED SAFFRON HALIBUT
WITH AVOCADO & TROPICAL FRUIT SALSA

INGREDIENTS

Fish

4	6-oz (175-g) halibut fillets	4
to taste	kosher salt and freshly ground black pepper	to taste
1 tsp	ground cumin	5 mL
½ tsp	turmeric	2 mL
pinch	saffron threads, crumbled	pinch
pinch	cayenne pepper	pinch
1	lime, cut in half	1
	extra virgin olive oil	
1	plank (cedar or fruitwood), soaked overnight or at least 1 hour	1

continues on next page

METHOD

Fish

Season both sides of the fillets with salt and pepper. Combine the cumin, turmeric, saffron, and cayenne and sprinkle evenly over the fillets. Squeeze the cut lime over the fillets and drizzle them with a little olive oil. Marinate for 15 minutes.

Preheat the grill on medium-high for 5 or 10 minutes or until the chamber temperature rises above 500°F (260°C). Rinse the plank and place it on the cooking grate. Cover the grill and heat the plank for 4 or 5 minutes, or until it starts to throw off a bit of smoke and crackles lightly. Reduce the heat to medium-low.

Place the fillets on the plank and cook for 15 to 20 minutes or until the fish has an internal temperature of 135°F (57°C). Remove from the grill and tent lightly in foil. Let rest for 2 or 3 minutes while you make the salsa.

Salsa

2 cups	diced tropical fruit (any combination of mango, papaya, kiwi, and pineapple)	500 mL
2	just-ripe avocados, pitted, peeled, and coarsely chopped	2
3 Tbsp	chopped cilantro	45 mL
3 Tbsp	chopped red onion	45 mL
1	jalapeño chili, seeded and finely chopped	1
1	lime, juice of	1
pinch	sugar	pinch
to taste	kosher salt and freshly ground pepper	to taste

Salsa

In a bowl, gently toss the salsa ingredients. Taste and season with salt and pepper. Serve the fillets topped with a dollop of salsa, and serve the remaining salsa on the side.

The fruitiness and sweetness from the mangoes and spiciness from the cayenne, ginger, and pepper complement the halibut beautifully. Serves 4

GRILLED HALIBUT
WITH MANGO-GINGER SAUCE

INGREDIENTS

Mango-Ginger Sauce

2	mangoes, peeled and pitted	2
2	cloves garlic, minced	2
1 Tbsp	fresh lemon juice	15 mL
1 Tbsp	Dijon mustard	15 mL
1 tsp	minced fresh ginger	5 mL
dash	Worcestershire sauce	dash
to taste	salt and pepper	to taste

Fish

4	halibut steaks	4
pinch	each freshly ground pepper, seasoning salt, and cayenne	pinch

METHOD

To make the sauce, purée the sauce ingredients in a food processor or blender. Pour into a saucepan and set aside while you cook the halibut.

Rinse the halibut in cold water and pat dry. (Leave the skins on to hold the fish together on the grill.) Season the steaks with pepper, seasoning salt, and cayenne. Grill on low heat for 15 minutes per side, until the flesh is flaky. Keep warm.

Gently heat the sauce over low heat (don't boil). Arrange the halibut on plates and pour the sauce over top.

The lemon grass sticks provide a unique way to serve the halibut. If lemon grass isn't available, use metal skewers or proceed without cubing the fish. *Serves 6/Makes 12 skewers*

HALIBUT
ON LEMON GRASS STICKS

INGREDIENTS

6 Tbsp	Balkan-style yogurt	90 mL
4 Tbsp	fresh lemon juice	60 mL
1 tsp	smoked Spanish paprika	5 mL
½ tsp	ground cumin	2 mL
1 tsp	garam masala	5 mL
1 tsp	fresh ginger, minced	5 mL
2	cloves garlic, minced	2
to taste	sea salt	to taste
to taste	freshly ground black pepper, preferably Malabar or Tellicherry	to taste
2 Tbsp	grapeseed oil	30 mL
½ tsp	ground cardamom	2 mL
2 lb	halibut fillets, cut into 2-inch (5-cm) cubes	1 kg
3	bunches lemon grass	3
for garnish	lime wedges	for garnish

METHOD

Mix together all the ingredients, except for the halibut, lime wedges, and lemon grass. Stir well to combine. Add the halibut to the marinade, stirring to ensure that it's coated evenly. Cover and chill for 30 minutes.

Trim the lemon grass and peel back until you have just the stiff center left. Cut into lengths of about 5 inches (12 cm). When the fish has marinated, thread 3 pieces on each lemon grass stick.

Heat a ribbed griddle to high heat and brush on a little oil. Grill the skewered halibut for about 2 minutes per side or until cooked through. Serve on a platter garnished with lime wedges.

CAREN'S TIP

Yogurt is a great tenderizer. Because of that property, don't let the fish sit in the marinade for longer than 1 hour or it will become mushy.

This one doesn't heat up the house, doesn't take any time, and is awesome for its simplicity. To add a little green to the plates, steam some asparagus, broccoli, or snow peas. Basmati rice, steamed green vegetables, and grilled pineapple slices complete the meal. Serves 4

HALIBUT
WITH MANGO SAUCE

INGREDIENTS

Fish.

1 Tbsp	puréed ginger root	15 mL
1	orange, zest only	1
1 Tbsp	minced fresh thyme	15 mL
1 Tbsp	canola oil	15 mL
to taste	freshly ground black pepper	to taste
4	5-oz (150-g) halibut fillets	4

continues on next page

METHOD

Combine the ginger, orange zest, thyme, oil, and pepper. Spread evenly over both sides of the halibut fillets. Let stand for 10 minutes while the grill is heating. Grill on medium-high heat for about 8 minutes, or until the fish is just done and flaky in the center. Pool some mango sauce on each plate and place a piece of grilled halibut on top.

Mango Sauce

Peel, pit, and purée the mangoes. Add the remaining ingredients, thinning the sauce with additional orange juice if needed. Taste the finished sauce and balance the flavors with salt and hot chili flakes.

Mango Sauce

Makes 1½ cups (375 mL)

2–3	ripe mangoes	2–3
2 Tbsp	puréed ginger root	30 mL
2	oranges, juice and zest	2
¼ cup	white wine	60 mL
2 Tbsp	minced red bell pepper (optional)	30 mL
1–2 Tbsp	honey to taste	15–30 mL
2 Tbsp	minced fresh thyme	30 mL
1 Tbsp	minced parsley	15 mL
to taste	salt and hot chili flakes	to taste

DEE'S TIP

Mango sauce can be frozen if you leave out the fresh herbs, adding them after thawing.

The flavor of the simply seasoned halibut is accented by the colorful Mediterranean-style salad, flavored with garlic, fresh herbs, and extra virgin olive oil. Use green beans instead of wax beans, or use a combination of the two. A mix of small, different-colored tomatoes makes the salad even more colorful. Serves 4

GRILLED HALIBUT FILLETS
WITH WAX BEAN & ROMA TOMATO SALAD

INGREDIENTS

Salad

4	ripe Roma or plum tomatoes, cut into wedges	4
½ lb	wax beans, trimmed and blanched	250 g
½	small red onion, thinly sliced	½
16–20	black olives, whole	16–20
1	clove garlic, crushed	1
3 Tbsp	extra virgin olive oil	45 mL
3 Tbsp	balsamic vinegar	45 mL
2 Tbsp	chopped fresh oregano or basil	30 mL
to taste	salt and freshly ground black pepper	to taste

continues on next page

METHOD

Salad

Combine all the ingredients in a bowl and toss gently. Cover and store in the refrigerator until the halibut is ready.

Fish

Preheat the grill to medium-high. Brush the halibut with olive oil and season with salt and pepper. Lightly oil the grill if it isn't non-stick. Grill the fillets for 3 to 4 minutes per side, or until just cooked through.

To serve, mound the salad in the center of individual plates. Top with the halibut. Garnish with lemon wedges and oregano or basil sprigs.

Fish

4	5-oz (150-g) halibut fillets	4
2 Tbsp	olive oil	30 mL
to taste	salt and freshly ground black pepper	to taste
for garnish	lemon wedges and oregano or basil sprigs	for garnish

ERIC'S TIP

To blanch the wax beans, cook them in boiling water for 2 minutes. Drain well, plunge into ice-cold water, and then drain well again.

Thick halibut steaks are easy to grill and very classy to serve with this simple sauce. A salad of tiny tomatoes and miniature bocconcini complements the dish perfectly. Serves 4

GRILLED HALIBUT
WITH TAPENADE DRIZZLE
& TOMATO & BOCCONCINI SALAD

INGREDIENTS

Lemon Tapenade Drizzle

¼ cup	extra virgin olive oil	60 mL
1	clove garlic, crushed	1
2 Tbsp	freshly squeezed lemon juice	30 mL
¼ cup	pitted niçoise olives	60 mL
1 tsp	grated lemon zest	5 mL
1 tsp	granulated sugar	5 mL
¼ tsp	chili paste	1 mL
½ tsp	fish sauce	2 mL

Tomato & Bocconcini Salad

1 cup	grape tomatoes, halved	250 mL
¾ cup	mini fresh bocconcini cheese balls	175 mL
dash	extra virgin olive oil	dash
dash	reduced balsamic vinegar	dash
to taste	salt and freshly ground black pepper	to taste
for garnish	chopped fresh basil and/or Italian parsley	for garnish

METHOD

Lemon Tapenade Drizzle

Combine the oil, garlic, lemon juice, olives, lemon zest, sugar, chili paste, and fish sauce in a blender. Whirl at high speed until very smooth. Set aside.

Tomato & Bocconcini Salad

Combine the tomatoes and cheese in a bowl. Drizzle with a bit of olive oil and a few drops of reduced balsamic vinegar, then season with salt and pepper, and scatter the herbs over top. Set aside.

continues on next page

Fish

2 Tbsp	extra virgin olive oil	30 mL
1	clove garlic, crushed	1
1 tsp	finely grated lemon zest	5 mL
1 tsp	basil pesto	5 mL
to taste	salt and freshly ground black pepper	to taste
4	5–6-oz (120–150-g) pieces of halibut, about 1 inch (2.5 cm) thick	4

Fish

Combine the oil, garlic, lemon zest, pesto, salt, and pepper in a small bowl, then rub over both sides of the halibut. Heat the grill over high heat for 10 minutes. Clean the grill well, then brush with oil (the easiest way to do this is to soak a folded paper towel in canola oil, pick it up with tongs, and rub it over the grill racks). Grill the fish over direct heat until just opaque, about 4 minutes per side.

Remove from the grill and serve immediately, drizzled with the lemon tapenade, with the tomato salad on the side.

Influenced by Japanese cookery, this features sweet, salt, hot, and pickled all in one dish. Everything except grilling the fish can be done ahead, so the time until dinner is on the table just nudges my personal goal of half an hour. The flavors in this dish need little other than a pot of steamed basmati rice and some fresh asparagus or broccoli for accompaniment. Serves 4

HALIBUT ON WARM GREENS
WITH MISO-GARI VINAIGRETTE

INGREDIENTS

Fish

4	5-oz (150-g) halibut steaks	4
1 cup	Miso-Gari Vinaigrette	250 mL
2 bunches	bok choy or other mild Asian greens	2 bunches
4	blood oranges, tangerines, or mandarins, peeled and sliced	4
1 bunch	cilantro sprigs	1 bunch
1 Tbsp	sesame seeds	15 mL
	Pickled Red Onions*	

continues on next page

METHOD

Fish

Brush the halibut steaks with ¼ cup (60 mL) of the Miso-Gari Vinaigrette and set aside for 20 minutes. Meanwhile, wash and finely chop the bok choy. Don't spin dry! Preheat the grill to medium-high. Grill the halibut until just done in the center, about 7 minutes per 1 inch (2.5 cm) of thickness.

Toss the greens in a hot non-stick sauté pan over high heat until they wilt. Add the remaining Miso-Gari Vinaigrette and toss well. Top with the grilled halibut.

Garnish with the sliced citrus, cilantro, and a sprinkle of sesame seeds. Drape a few curls of Pickled Red Onion alongside.

Miso-Gari Vinaigrette
Makes about 2 cups (500 mL)

1–2 Tbsp	white miso	15–30 mL
¼ cup	soy sauce	60 mL
¼ cup	honey, warmed	60 mL
2 Tbsp	sesame oil	30 mL
2 Tbsp	minced cilantro	30 mL
3	green onions, finely minced	3
2 Tbsp	minced pickled ginger	30 mL
1 cup	Japanese rice vinegar	250 mL
1	lemon, juice and zest	1
to taste	salt and hot chili flakes	to taste

Pickled Red Onions*
Makes 8 cups (2 L)

4	red onions, thinly sliced	4
4 cups	boiling water	1 L
4 cups	mild white wine vinegar or rice vinegar	1 L
1 Tbsp	sugar	15 mL
1 tsp	salt	5 mL
½ tsp	dried thyme	2 mL
to taste	hot chili flakes	to taste

Miso-Gari Vinaigrette

Whisk the soy sauce into the miso until smooth. Whisk in the remaining ingredients. Best within 3 days of being made.

Pickled Red Onions

Place the onion slices in a colander in the sink. Pour the boiling water over them, discarding the water. While the onions are hot, transfer them to a glass or non-reactive bowl and add the remaining ingredients. Mix well, cover, and chill.

DEE'S TIP

Choose dark red onions for the most intense color. Store the pickled onions in the fridge for up to a week for optimal crunch. They're great on sandwiches, pizza, salads, risottos, or anything that calls for the crunch of tangy onion.

*I first met pickled onions through Deborah Madison, the gifted author of *The Greens Cookbook* and *The Savory Way*. My heartfelt thanks for her generosity in letting me use this recipe from *The Savory Way*.

The sweetness of the pear and fennel balanced with lemon goes well with the halibut. The teardrop or pear tomato is slightly smaller than a cherry tomato. They look good, but you can replace them with another kind of tomato if you prefer. Serves 4

GRILLED HALIBUT

ON A BED OF PEARS, FENNEL & TOMATOES

INGREDIENTS

1 Tbsp	olive oil	15 mL
4	8-oz (225-g) halibut fillets	4
1	fennel bulb, trimmed	1
2	pears, cored and sliced	2
½ lb	teardrop tomatoes, washed	250 g
1	lemon, juice of	1
1 Tbsp	golden corn syrup	15 mL
¼ cup	olive oil	60 mL
to taste	salt and freshly ground black pepper	to taste

METHOD

Rub the 1 Tbsp (15 mL) olive oil onto the halibut and set aside while the grill heats to medium-high.

Remove the outside layer and any brown layers from the fennel bulb. Cut the bulb in half lengthwise, remove the core and slice it thinly crosswise; transfer to a bowl. Slice the pears thick enough so they won't fall apart when they're tossed together. Add the tomatoes and pears to the fennel.

In a separate bowl, combine the lemon juice and corn syrup and whisk in the ¼ cup (60 mL) of olive oil. Season with salt and pepper. Add this dressing to the fennel mixture and toss well. Set aside.

Preheat the oven to 350°F (180°C). When grilling the halibut, make sure the grill is very clean and very hot before putting the fish on it. Use the grill just to quick-mark and flavor the fish, 1½ minutes on each side. Transfer the fillets to a baking dish and bake for 5 to 10 minutes in the oven or until cooked through.

Arrange the fennel mixture on a serving plate, lay the fish on top, and serve.

JUDY'S TIP

This recipe uses a common restaurant technique. Meat or fish is grilled to create grill marks then transferred to the oven to finish cooking. This ensures that the fish or meat doesn't become blackened on the outside from the high heat of the grill while remaining raw in the center.

You can do this on a barbecue by keeping one side of the barbecue turned off. When the fish is marked, move it to the cool side and keep the lid down to finish cooking.

This dish is a great combination of flavors and textures. If making your own mayonnaise doesn't appeal to you, just add the honey to ⅔ cup (150 mL) of store-bought mayonnaise. Serves 4

HALIBUT & BACON SKEWERS
WITH HONEYED MAYONNAISE

INGREDIENTS

Halibut & Bacon Skewers

1	lemon, juice of	1
¼ cup	extra virgin olive oil	60 mL
2	small onions	2
¼ lb	small mushrooms	125 g
to taste	sea salt and freshly ground black pepper	to taste
1½ lb	halibut fillets, cut into 1½-inch (4-cm) cubes	750 g
¼ lb	sliced bacon	125 g
8	cherry tomatoes	8

Mayonnaise

2 tsp	honey	10 mL
1	egg yolk	1
1 Tbsp	Dijon mustard	15 mL
1 Tbsp	lemon juice	15 mL
½ cup	extra virgin olive oil	125 mL
to taste	sea salt and freshly ground black pepper	to taste

METHOD

Combine the juice of one lemon and the olive oil. Cut the onions into wedges and place them in a bowl with the mushrooms. Toss with half the lemon mixture and season to taste. Add the remaining lemon mixture to the halibut and season to taste. Cut the bacon in half crosswise and roll up loosely.

Close to serving time, thread the fish, onions, and mushrooms onto skewers, adding the bacon rolls and tomatoes here and there. Grill for 10 minutes or so over medium-high heat until the halibut flakes. Serve with the mayonnaise.

Mayonnaise

For the mayonnaise, combine the honey, egg yolk, mustard, and 1 Tbsp (15 mL) lemon juice until smooth. Season to taste. Slowly beat in the oil to form an emulsion. You can do this by hand or with a hand blender, blender, or food processor.

HALIBUT PROVENÇAL | page 124

Michael Smith — Exclusive

PLANKED SAFFRON HALIBUT WITH AVOCADO
& TROPICAL FRUIT SALSA | pages 130–31

Ron Shewchuk — *Planking Secrets*

PHOTO BY GREG ATHANS • FOOD STYLING BY NATHAN FONG

PHOTO BY RYAN SULLIVAN, PURDY & CO. • FOOD STYLING BY MURRAY BANCROFT

GRILLED HALIBUT FILLETS WITH WAX BEANS
& ROMA TOMATO SALAD | page 136

Eric Akis — *Everyone Can Cook Seafood*

Serve these simple kebabs over saffron rice garnished with cherry tomatoes. Serves 5/Makes 10 kebabs

HALIBUT KEBABS

INGREDIENTS

Marinade

¼ cup	lemon juice	60 mL
¼ cup	grated onion	60 mL
¼ cup	olive oil	60 mL
1 tsp	salt	5 mL
½ tsp	freshly ground black pepper	2 mL

Kebabs

2 lb	halibut fillets, cut into 1-inch (2.5-cm) cubes	1 kg
50–60	bay leaves	50–60
10	medium metal or pre-soaked wooden skewers	10
¼ cup	melted butter for basting	60 mL
½ cup	chopped green onion	125 mL
¼ cup	chopped fresh parsley	60 mL
2	medium tomatoes, cut into 8 wedges	2
2	lemons, cut into wedges	2

METHOD

Combine the marinade ingredients in a non-reactive bowl. Toss the fish pieces and bay leaves gently in the marinade to coat. Cover and let stand for 2 hours at room temperature, stirring occasionally.

Remove the fish and bay leaves from the marinade and thread about 5 to 6 pieces of fish, alternating with bay leaves, onto each skewer. Grill the skewers over medium heat for 8 to 10 minutes, turning and basting frequently with melted butter.

Transfer the fish onto individual plates, garnish with green onion, parsley, tomato, and lemon wedges.

A colorful Pacific Northwest creation combining two popular fish of the Pacific coast.
Serves 4/Makes 8 kebabs

HALIBUT & SALMON KEBABS

INGREDIENTS

Marinade

¼ cup	olive oil	60 mL
¼ cup	lemon juice	60 mL
¼ cup	dry white wine	60 mL
1 Tbsp	finely chopped fresh dill	15 mL
1 Tbsp	grated lemon zest	15 mL
1 tsp	garlic paste	5 mL
1 tsp	red pepper flakes	5 mL
1 tsp	sugar	5 mL
½ tsp	salt	2 mL
½ tsp	freshly ground black pepper	2 mL
	vegetable oil for basting	

Kebabs

1 lb	skinless salmon fillet	500 g
1 lb	skinless halibut fillet	500 g
8	cherry tomatoes	8
8	medium metal or pre-soaked wooden skewers	8

METHOD

Combine all the marinade ingredients in a non-reactive bowl.

Cut the salmon and halibut fillets into 1-inch (2.5-cm) cubes, add to the marinade, and toss gently to coat. Cover and marinate in the refrigerator for 2 hours.

Drain the marinade and reserve. Thread 3 to 4 pieces of halibut, alternating with salmon, onto each skewer. Top each skewer with a cherry tomato. Brush liberally with reserved marinade.

Grill over medium heat for 2 minutes on each side. Baste with the marinade and grill both sides an additional minute, basting liberally at each turn, until both fish are opaque.

For a gorgeous, colorful presentation, serve over saffron rice garnished with cherry tomatoes.

Halibut is such a delicately flavored fish that you don't want to do much to it. The key here is to use the very freshest ingredients. This dish is excellent with rice and your favorite salad. Serves 4

DILLED & GRILLED HALIBUT STEAKS

INGREDIENTS

4	6-oz (175-g) fresh halibut fillets, skin on	4
to taste	kosher salt and freshly ground black pepper	to taste
¼ cup	fresh dill, chopped	60 mL
1	lemon, juice of	1
	extra virgin olive oil	
for garnish	lemon wedges	for garnish

METHOD

Place the fish fillet in a non-reactive dish or baking pan. Season both sides with salt and pepper and coat evenly with the dill. Squeeze lemon over the fish and then drizzle generously with the olive oil to coat. Let sit for 15 minutes. Meanwhile, prepare the grill for direct medium heat.

Place the halibut pieces on the grill, skin side down. Cook for about 6 minutes until just cooked through, to an internal temperature of about 140 to 150°F (60 to 65°C). Remove from the grill (the skin will stick to the grill but should easily separate from the fish) and let rest for a couple of minutes. To serve, season with a little more salt and pepper, drizzle with olive oil, and accompany with lemon wedges.

This dish is at its best when local corn and tomatoes are in season and bursting with fresh flavor. Tiny new potatoes, boiled or steamed, go nicely with this dish. If fresh corn is unavailable, use ½ cup (125 mL) of frozen corn kernels. Serves 2

FOIL-BARBECUED HALIBUT
WITH CORN, TOMATOES & DILL

INGREDIENTS

2 Tbsp	olive oil, divided	30 mL
2	5-oz (150-g) halibut fillets, trimmed	2
to taste	salt and freshly ground black pepper	to taste
1	cob corn, kernels removed	1
2	ripe medium tomatoes, chopped	2
2	cloves garlic, thinly sliced	2
¼ cup	dry white wine	60 mL
1 Tbsp	chopped fresh dill	15 mL

METHOD

Preheat the barbecue to medium. Cut and overlap 2 pieces of foil, each 18 × 12 inches (45 × 30 cm). Brush the top of the foil with 1 Tbsp (15 mL) of the oil. Place the fillets in the center, about 2 inches (5 cm) apart. Drizzle with the remaining olive oil and season with salt and pepper.

Combine the corn kernels, tomatoes, garlic, wine, and dill in a bowl. Spoon the mixture over the fish. Fold the foil over the fish and seal the top. Grill for 12 to 15 minutes, or until the fish is just cooked through. Serve directly from the foil, or transfer to individual serving plates.

Olive oil, oregano, mozzarella, and tomato give these fish burgers a pleasing taste of Italy. Instead of grilling the fish, pan-fry for a similar length of time in a non-stick skillet over medium-high heat. Finish as described in the recipe. Serves 4

ITALIAN-STYLE HALIBUT BURGERS

INGREDIENTS

4	¼-lb (125-g) boneless, skinless halibut fillets	4
2 Tbsp	olive oil	30 mL
½ tsp	paprika	2 mL
1 tsp	dried oregano	5 mL
to taste	salt and freshly ground black pepper	to taste
1¼ cups	tomato-based pasta sauce, heated	310 mL
4	slices mozzarella cheese	4
4	panini or hamburger buns, warmed	4
4	lettuce leaves	4

METHOD

Preheat the grill to medium-high. Brush the halibut fillets with the olive oil; sprinkle with the paprika, oregano, salt, and pepper. Grill for 2 to 3 minutes per side. Top each piece of fish with a spoonful of the pasta sauce and a slice of mozzarella cheese. When the cheese is melted and the fish is cooked through, cut the panini or hamburger buns in half. Place a lettuce leaf on the bottom of each bun, top with a piece of halibut, and replace the top halves of the buns. Serve the remaining pasta sauce in a small bowl alongside for dipping the burgers in.

You can use milder jalapeños, or hotter serrano chilies for this dish. Serves 6

CHILI & ROCK SALT GRILLED HALIBUT

INGREDIENTS

2	green chilies, finely chopped	2
to taste	coarse-grained salt	to taste
6	6-oz (175-g) fresh halibut fillets, skin on	6

METHOD

Preheat a charcoal or gas barbecue to low heat. Mash the chilies and salt together to form a paste. Coat the halibut fillets with the paste. Place the halibut fillets, skin side down, on the grill. Grill until each side is golden brown, about 7 minutes per side.

Serve with steamed new potatoes and asparagus.

JAMIE'S TIP

If working with a charcoal barbecue, wait until the barbecue has burned down to a nice slow fire.

SIMPLE MARINADES
& SAUCES

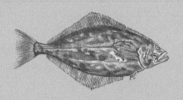

FISHING GEAR

The gear for fishing halibut is comprised of
units of leaded ground line in lengths of
100 fathoms (600 feet) called skates.
Each skate has roughly 100 hooks attached to it.
The lines with the hooks attached are called gangens.
These gangens are tied or snapped on to the
ground line. A set consists of one or more baited skates,
joined together, laid on the ocean floor, and anchored at
each end. The ends have a float line and a buoy
attached. Bait is typically frozen herring, octopus,
or other fish. Depending on the time of year,
fishing ground, depth, and bait, a set may be left
undisturbed for 2 to 20 hours before being removed
from the water, normally by a hydraulic puller.
On the boat, the halibut are cleaned and packed
with ice to retain freshness.

᠔

This versatile sauce can be used as a marinade as well as a sauce. Use just enough to coat the halibut, and don't leave the halibut marinating for any longer than an hour. Makes 1 cup (250 mL)

CHARMOULA SAUCE

INGREDIENTS

¼ cup	olive oil	60 mL
¼ cup	lemon juice	60 mL
½ cup	finely chopped cilantro leaves	125 mL
½ cup	finely chopped parsley	125 mL
2 Tbsp	ground cumin	30 mL
2 tsp	paprika	10 mL
1	hot red chili, seeded (optional)	1
½ tsp	ground ginger	2 mL
½ tsp	dried marjoram	2 mL
½ tsp	freshly ground black pepper	2 mL
½ tsp	salt	2 mL

METHOD

Combine all the ingredients in a food processor and blend into a smooth paste. Adjust the seasoning; if you prefer a hotter version, add cayenne pepper according to taste. Store in a jar in the refrigerator until needed.

For a hotter version, add 2 seeded scotch bonnet or jalapeño peppers while blending. Use just enough to coat the halibut, and don't leave the halibut marinating for any longer than an hour. Makes 1 cup (250 mL)

JERK PASTE

INGREDIENTS

1	medium onion, coarsely chopped	1
2	green onions, coarsely chopped	2
3 Tbsp	soy sauce	45 mL
2 Tbsp	white vinegar	30 mL
2 Tbsp	lime juice	30 mL
2 Tbsp	dark rum	30 mL
2 Tbsp	brown sugar	30 mL
2 tsp	freshly ground black pepper	10 mL
1 tsp	garlic paste	5 mL
1 tsp	ginger paste	5 mL
1 tsp	dried sage	5 mL
1 tsp	dried allspice	5 mL
1 tsp	dried thyme	5 mL
1 tsp	hot red pepper flakes	5 mL
1 tsp	salt	5 mL
½ tsp	ground cinnamon	2 mL
½ tsp	ground nutmeg	2 mL
3 Tbsp	olive oil	45 mL

METHOD

Process all the ingredients, except the olive oil, in a blender. When a smooth purée forms, gradually add the olive oil and continue blending into a smooth paste. Cover and store in a jar in the refrigerator until needed.

This can be used as a marinade or a sauce. Use just enough to coat the halibut, and don't leave the halibut marinating for any longer than an hour. Makes 2 cups (500 mL)

TERIYAKI SAUCE

INGREDIENTS

1 cup	soy sauce	250 mL
⅔ cup	sake	150 mL
⅓ cup	mirin (sweet rice wine)	75 mL
⅓ cup	sugar	75 mL
1 Tbsp	grated fresh ginger	15 mL
3	cloves garlic, crushed	3
1	orange, cut into wedges (leave peel on)	1

METHOD

Boil all the ingredients until reduced by 20 percent.

Remove the orange pieces.

With its creamy texture and subtle flavor, this sauce is wonderful with halibut. Makes about 1½ cups (375 mL)

COCONUT GINGER SAUCE

INGREDIENTS

1 Tbsp	peanut or canola oil	15 mL
2 tsp	chopped shallots	10 mL
2 tsp	chopped fresh ginger	10 mL
1 cup	coconut milk	250 mL
2 Tbsp	soy sauce	30 mL
2 Tbsp	palm or brown sugar	30 mL
1 Tbsp	lime juice	15 mL
1 tsp	lime zest	5 mL
2 Tbsp	chopped basil	30 mL

METHOD

Heat the oil over medium heat in a small pot. Add the shallots and ginger and cook until they sizzle. Add the remaining ingredients, except the basil, and simmer for 20 minutes over low heat. Add the basil just before serving.

This sauce has a mild ginger flavor that's perfect with halibut. Makes about 1 cup (250 mL)

GINGER CREAM SAUCE

INGREDIENTS

2 Tbsp	butter	30 mL
2 Tbsp	peanut or canola oil	30 mL
2 Tbsp	chopped shallots	30 mL
2 Tbsp	chopped garlic	30 mL
¼ cup	fresh ginger, peeled and finely chopped	60 mL
½ cup	dry white wine	125 mL
1 Tbsp	fish sauce	15 mL
2 tsp	ground white pepper	10 mL
¾ cup	coconut milk	175 mL
1¼ cups	whipping cream	310 mL

METHOD

Heat the butter and oil in a saucepan over high heat. Add the shallots and garlic and sauté for 2 minutes. Add the ginger and sauté, stirring, for 2 minutes. Add the wine, fish sauce, and white pepper. Bring to a boil, then reduce the heat to medium and cook, stirring, for 3 minutes.

Add the coconut milk and whipping cream. Increase the heat to high and bring to a boil. Reduce the heat to low and simmer until it's reduced by half, about 5 minutes. Strain the sauce through a fine sieve and keep warm until serving time.

This can also be served with sole, cod, red snapper, or salmon. The mixture of tarragon and lemon juice gives this sauce its zest. Makes 1 cup (250 mL)

TARRAGON FISH SAUCE

INGREDIENTS

3 Tbsp	butter	45 mL
⅔ cup	whipping cream	150 mL
3 Tbsp	finely chopped tarragon	45 mL
1 Tbsp	freshly squeezed lemon juice	15 mL
to taste	freshly ground black pepper	to taste

METHOD

Melt the butter in a saucepan. Add the whipping cream and simmer until the cream has thickened. Add the tarragon and lemon juice and stir. Season with pepper. Heat gently for 2 to 3 minutes. Pour over cooked fish.

A classic sauce that's great over halibut, steaks, roast beef, and even the lowly hamburger. Makes about 1 cup (250 mL)

TARRAGON BLENDER BÉARNAISE

INGREDIENTS

¼ cup	tarragon vinegar	60 mL
2 Tbsp	minced shallots	30 mL
2 Tbsp	finely chopped tarragon	30 mL
¼ tsp	white pepper	1 mL
3	large egg yolks	3
1 cup	melted butter, cooled slightly	250 mL

METHOD

Mix together the vinegar, shallots, tarragon, and pepper in a small saucepan. Cook over high heat until the mixture has reduced to 1 to 2 Tbsp (15 to 30 mL). Transfer the contents of the saucepan to a blender or food processor. Add the egg yolks and process briefly. With the machine running, slowly add the cooled melted butter in a steady stream and blend until the mixture thickens. Serve immediately or keep warm over hot water.

This sauce has a sweet and sour flavor that's great with halibut. Makes 1½ cups (375 mL)

SWEET HOT TAMARIND SAUCE

INGREDIENTS

2 Tbsp	peanut or canola oil	30 mL
1	small onion, diced	1
4	cloves garlic, finely diced	4
1 tsp	red curry paste	5 mL
4	red chilies, thinly sliced	4
2 Tbsp	chopped cilantro stems	30 mL
¼ cup	palm or brown sugar	60 mL
1 cup	tamarind water	250 mL
1 Tbsp	soy sauce	15 mL

METHOD

Heat the oil in a saucepan over medium heat and fry the onion, garlic, and curry paste for 2 minutes. Add the chilies, cilantro, sugar, tamarind water, and soy sauce and bring to a boil. Lower the heat to a simmer and cook for 10 minutes. This sauce will keep in the fridge for up to 3 days and can be served hot or cold.

NATHAN'S TIP

To make tamarind water, break off one sixth of a brick of tamarind pulp and cover with ½ cup (125 mL) boiling water. Let sit until cool. Work the tamarind with your fingers, until it dissolves into the water. Press through a sieve and discard what remains in the sieve. Add additional water to make 1 cup (250 mL).

This is light, but has a very rich flavor. Makes 1 cup (250 mL)

NAMI SAUCE

INGREDIENTS

4 Tbsp	soy sauce	60 mL
4 Tbsp	mirin (sweet rice wine)	60 mL
2 Tbsp	rice vinegar	30 mL
⅓ cup	Japanese roasted sesame sauce (tahini will work if you can't find the Japanese product)	75 mL
2 tsp	sugar	10 mL
2 Tbsp	roasted sesame seeds	30 mL
2 Tbsp	roasted sesame seeds (optional)	30 mL

METHOD

Blend all the ingredients well with a whisk. Pour the sauce over the cooked halibut. If you like, sprinkle the additional sesame seeds on top.

Delicious served with broiled or baked halibut. Makes 2 cups (500 mL)

ROASTED GARLIC AÏOLI

INGREDIENTS

2 cups	quality mayonnaise	500 mL
1	whole garlic bulb	1
½ tsp	olive oil	2 mL
½ tsp	rosemary or thyme	2 mL
to taste	salt and pepper	to taste

METHOD

Cut off the top of the garlic bulb to expose a little of the flesh. Lay on a piece of tin foil and drizzle the olive oil and rosemary or thyme over the bulb. Season with salt and pepper. Wrap the foil around the garlic to form a package. Roast in a 325°F (160°C) oven for 30 to 40 minutes. Squeeze the garlic flesh out of the skins and mash in a bowl with a fork to form a smooth paste. Whisk in the mayonnaise until blended. Season with salt and pepper to taste.

This sauce is a snap to make and can be used as a dipping sauce with halibut, as well as cold poached shrimp. Sweet chili sauce is available at your local supermarket. Makes ½ cup (125 mL)

COCKTAIL SAUCE

INGREDIENTS

½ cup	sweet chili sauce	125 mL
2 Tbsp	ketchup	30 mL
1 tsp	prepared horseradish	5 mL
½ tsp	Worcestershire sauce	2 mL
1 tsp	fresh lemon juice	5 mL

METHOD

Combine all the ingredients and mix well. Cover and chill for 30 minutes before serving. The sauce can be stored in an airtight container in the refrigerator for up to 2 weeks.

Good with either hot or cold halibut—try it with cold, flaked halibut as a sandwich filling—or on a halibut burger. Makes 1 cup (250 mL)

HORSERADISH SEAFOOD SAUCE

INGREDIENTS

½ cup	chili sauce	125 mL
½ cup	mayonnaise	125 mL
2 Tbsp	grated fresh horseradish or horseradish-vinegar mixture	30 mL
dash	hot pepper sauce	dash
to taste	freshly ground black pepper	to taste

METHOD

Mix the ingredients together in a bowl and serve with seafood.

This keeps well in the refrigerator, although the fresh herbs will darken and soften after a few days. Aside from using it as a sauce for halibut, you can use it as a dip, a spread for sandwiches, a garnish for grilled vegetables, and a flavoring for grains and gratins. Use either blanched or unblanched almonds.

Makes about 1 cup (250 mL)

SAFFRON ALMOND SAUCE

INGREDIENTS

2 cups	sliced almonds, toasted	500 mL
pinch	saffron	pinch
1	orange, juice and zest	1
1 Tbsp	olive oil	15 mL
4–6	cloves garlic, minced	4–6
½	onion, finely chopped (optional)	½
1 Tbsp	minced fresh oregano	15 mL
1 Tbsp	minced parsley	15 mL
1	lemon, juice of	1
to taste	salt and cayenne	to taste

METHOD

Grind the nuts in a food processor and leave them there. Combine the saffron, orange juice and zest in a small pot and simmer on low heat for several minutes. In a small frying pan, heat the oil to medium hot, add the garlic and onion, if desired, and cook until tender and beginning to color. Combine with the nuts and grind as finely or coarsely as you like. Add the herbs and saffron with orange juice, and adjust the flavor with the lemon juice, salt, and cayenne. Pulse to combine.

Thin with water to the desired consistency. For a dip, leave it thick; for a sauce or baste, add a little more water. Store in the refrigerator.

Rather than pounding the ingredients together as is traditional, my quick version of this classic sauce is blended in a food processor. Makes 1¼ cups (310 mL)

QUICK ROUILLE

INGREDIENTS

1	roasted red bell pepper, sliced (see page 17)	1
2	cloves garlic, coarsely chopped	2
1	slice white bread, torn into pieces	1
¾ cup	mayonnaise	175 mL
to taste	salt, freshly ground black pepper, cayenne pepper, and lemon juice	to taste

METHOD

Place all the ingredients in a food processor and process until smooth. Place in a bowl, cover, and allow the flavors to meld in the refrigerator for several hours.

Salsa verde (green sauce) is an Italian-style sauce that can lift the flavor of any kind of fish.
Makes ¾ cup (175 mL)

SALSA VERDE

INGREDIENTS

¼ cup	chopped fresh parsley	60 mL
¼ cup	capers, finely chopped	60 mL
4	anchovy fillets, mashed	4
2	cloves garlic, finely chopped	2
1 tsp	Dijon mustard	5 mL
1 tsp	red wine vinegar	5 mL
½ cup	extra virgin olive oil	125 mL
to taste	salt and freshly ground black pepper	to taste

METHOD

Combine the parsley, capers, anchovies, garlic, mustard, and vinegar in a bowl. Slowly beat in the olive oil. Season with salt and pepper. Cover and set aside at room temperature. Leftover salsa verde can be stored in a sealed jar in the fridge for a week or so. Bring to room temperature before serving.

This Greek-style sauce tastes great on halibut. If you don't have fresh herbs, substitute ½ tsp (2 mL) dried.
Makes 1¼ cups (310 mL)

TZATZIKI SAUCE

INGREDIENTS

½ cup	yogurt	125 mL
¼ cup	sour cream	60 mL
½	English cucumber, coarsely grated and moisture squeezed out	½
2	cloves garlic, chopped	2
1 Tbsp	chopped fresh dill	15 mL
1 Tbsp	chopped fresh mint	15 mL
to taste	salt, freshly ground black pepper, and lemon juice	to taste

METHOD

Combine all the ingredients in a bowl. Cover and allow the flavors to meld in the refrigerator for several hours before serving.

This yellow, lemony, dill-flecked sauce can be made ahead of time and refrigerated for up to 5 days. It goes well with all kinds of seafood, such as crab, shrimp, or cold salmon. Makes 1½ cups (375 mL)

MUSTARD DILL SAUCE

INGREDIENTS

1	egg, plus 1 egg yolk, at room temperature	1
2 Tbsp	fresh lemon juice	30 mL
2 Tbsp	sugar	30 mL
2 Tbsp	Dijon mustard	30 mL
1 Tbsp	grated lemon rind	15 mL
½ cup	chopped dill, fresh or frozen	125 mL
1 cup	safflower oil	250 mL

METHOD

Blend the egg and yolk in a food processor until creamy. Add the lemon juice, sugar, mustard, lemon rind, and dill. Process until smooth. Add the oil in a slow, thin stream, with the motor running. The mixture should thicken. Refrigerate if not used immediately.

An excellent flavoring agent, garlic butter can be brushed on halibut and other fish, chicken, vegetables, and of course crusty bread. It can be frozen inside a roll of aluminum foil or in little crocks, which make good gifts for garlic lovers. Makes 2½ cups (625 mL)

GARLIC BUTTER

INGREDIENTS

4–6	cloves garlic, peeled and dropped in boiling water for 2 minutes	4–6
1 lb	butter	500 g
½ cup	chopped parsley (optional)	125 mL
1 Tbsp	prepared horseradish	15 mL
1 Tbsp	Dijon mustard	15 mL

METHOD

Process the garlic cloves in a food processor. Add the butter in chunks and process until soft and creamy. Add the remaining ingredients and blend well. Place the butter on a piece of foil and form it into a roll. Freeze and cut off pieces as needed.

Use this on practically any fish. It melts on the cooked fish for an instant sauce and tastes good on vegetables too. Makes ½ cup (125 mL)

PARSLEY LEMON BUTTER

INGREDIENTS

½ cup	butter	125 mL
2 Tbsp	fresh lemon juice	30 mL
3 Tbsp	finely chopped parsley	45 mL
dash	hot pepper sauce	dash

METHOD

Mash all the ingredients by hand or in a food processor. Put in a pretty crock, cover with plastic wrap, and refrigerate. The butter will keep a few weeks in the refrigerator or it can be frozen.

Because it's served in small amounts—usually a thin shaving on grilled or broiled foods—the flavors of compound butters should be big. Choose a tart apple; its flavor will come through in the butter. If you use an organic red-skinned apple, cook it with the peel on for a pretty pink tint. If the grill isn't already on, slide the apple slices under the broiler or simply sauté them at high heat until the apple begins to soften. Makes ½ lb (250 g)

GRILLED APPLE-GARI BUTTER

INGREDIENTS

1	apple, peeled, cored, and sliced in eighths	1
4 Tbsp	minced gari (see sidebar)	60 mL
1	lemon, juice and zest	1
4 Tbsp	minced cilantro	60 mL
4	green onions, minced	4
to taste	salt and hot chili flakes	to taste
½ lb	unsalted butter, softened	250 g

METHOD

Grill, broil, or sauté the apple slices until they're soft. Chop or purée them finely. Combine the chopped apple with all the remaining ingredients. Divide into 3 or 4 equal amounts and wrap each separately in plastic wrap. Using the back of a metal spatula, form the compound butter into even logs ½ inch (1 cm) in diameter. Wrap in foil, label with the contents, date, and freeze until needed.

GARI OR PICKLED GINGER

Gari can be found in Asian markets, and just as easily made at home. Peel and thinly slice fresh ginger, preferably young new ginger in its tender pink skin, and immerse the slices in sweet Japanese rice vinegar seasoned with salt and a whiff of hot chili flakes. Put the jar away in the refrigerator for a few weeks, then add slivers to vinaigrettes, bean dishes, grains, Asian sauces ...

Excellent with grilled halibut. Cooked black beans and chopped fresh tomatoes make a nice addition—adding one additional cup to this recipe makes a great salad. Makes 4 cups (1 L)

ROASTED CORN
& RED PEPPER SALSA

INGREDIENTS

2 cups	frozen corn	500 mL
2 Tbsp	olive oil	30 mL
1 Tbsp	brown sugar	15 mL
1 cup	roasted red pepper, diced (see page 17)	250 mL
½ cup	red onion, diced	125 mL
⅓ cup	cilantro, chopped	75 mL
2	limes, juice and zest	2
1 tsp	cumin	5 mL
1 tsp	chili powder	5 mL

METHOD

In a baking dish, toss the corn in olive oil and brown sugar, and roast in a 350°F (180°C) oven until caramelized, about 20 minutes. Remove from the oven and add the remaining ingredients. Mix well and keep covered in the refrigerator.

This beautiful salsa will look even prettier if you try to dice the mango, papaya, red pepper, and red onion in small, even pieces. Makes 3 cups (750 mL)

PAPAYA MANGO SALSA

INGREDIENTS

1	mango, diced	1
1	papaya, diced	1
2	red peppers, diced	2
½	red onion, diced	½
1	jalapeño pepper, seeded and finely diced	1
1 cup	cilantro, chopped	250 mL
1 tsp	cumin	5 mL
1 tsp	chili powder	5 mL
1	lime, juice and zest	1
½ tsp	salt	2 mL

METHOD

In a large mixing bowl, mix together all the ingredients.

Store in the refrigerator for up to 2 days.

Any student of barbecue has to bow in the direction of Kansas City once in a while, as Paul Kirk is one of the world's greatest barbecue cooks and perhaps its best-known ambassador. Paul has taught thousands of cooks the essentials of barbecue, and this rich, sweet, tangy sauce is based on his Kansas City classic. Makes about 6 cups (1.5 L)

SATISFYING DIPPING SAUCE

INGREDIENTS

2 Tbsp	powdered ancho, poblano, or New Mexico chilies	30 mL
1 Tbsp	ground black pepper	15 mL
1 Tbsp	dry mustard	15 mL
1 tsp	ground coriander	5 mL
1 tsp	ground allspice	5 mL
¼ tsp	ground cloves	1 mL
½ tsp	grated nutmeg	2 mL
1 tsp	cayenne pepper	5 mL
¼ cup	canola oil	60 mL
1	onion, finely chopped	1
6	cloves garlic, finely chopped	6
1	shallot, minced	1
½ cup	tightly packed dark brown sugar	125 mL
1 cup	white vinegar	250 mL
½ cup	clover honey	125 mL
¼ cup	Worcestershire sauce, soy sauce, or a combination	60 mL

INGREDIENTS — continued

| 1 tsp | liquid smoke or hickory smoked salt (optional) | 5 mL |
| 4 cups | ketchup | 1 L |

METHOD

Mix all the spices together and set aside. Heat the oil in a big pot over medium heat and gently sauté the onion, garlic, and shallot until tender. Add the spices and mix thoroughly, cooking for 2 or 3 minutes to bring out their flavors. Add the remaining ingredients and simmer the mixture for 30 minutes, stirring often (be careful, it spatters). Don't cook it too long or it will start to caramelize and you'll have spicy fudge. If you want a very smooth sauce, blend with a hand blender or food processor. Preserve as you would a jam or jelly in mason jars.

Fish stock shouldn't be cooked for a long time, as overcooking will make the stock bitter. I usually keep a bag in the freezer and toss in bones until there's enough for a batch of stock. It can be difficult to collect enough bones to make fish stock, but your local fishmonger will have some to supplement your collection.

Makes about 4 cups (1 L)

FISH STOCK

INGREDIENTS

2 lb	fish bones and heads (shrimp shells add excellent flavor; halibut is a good all-purpose fish)	1 kg
10	whole black peppercorns	10
1	large onion, coarsely chopped	1
1	carrot, chopped	1
1	stalk celery, leaves included, roughly chopped	1
2	bunches parsley	2
1	lemon, quartered	1
3–4	sprigs fresh herbs (thyme, tarragon, savory, marjoram, dill, or fennel tops)	3–4
1 cup	white wine (optional)	250 mL
to taste	kosher salt	to taste

METHOD

Place all the ingredients, except the salt, in a large, heavy pot and cover with cold water filling 1 inch (2.5 cm) above the ingredients. Bring to a boil over high heat and skim if necessary. Reduce the heat and simmer, uncovered, for about 45 minutes, pressing the bones against the side of the pot every 15 minutes or so. Strain the stock and discard the solids. Return the stock to the pot and simmer for another 15 to 20 minutes to reduce the liquid. Season with salt.

ELLEN'S TIP

Use mostly raw fish and bones. You can supplement with cooked bones left over from a dinner, but they shouldn't make up most of the 2 lb (1 kg) you need for this recipe.

INDEX